Stinky, the Skunk That Wouldn't Leave

and Other Strange and Wonderful Animal Stories

Compiled and edited by
Joe L. Wheeler

Pacific Press® Publishing Association
Nampa, Idaho
Oshawa, Ontario, Canada
www.pacificpress.com

Cover art by Lars Justinen
Cover designed by Justinen Creative Group
Interior illustrations from the library of Joe L. Wheeler
Inside design by Kristin Hansen-Mellish

The author assumes full responsibility for the accuracy of all facts and quotations as cited in this book.

Additional copies of this book are available by calling toll-free 1-800-765-6955 or by visiting www.adventistbookcenter.com.

www.joewheelerbooks.com

Representing the author is WordServe Literary Group Ltd., 10152 Knoll Circle, Highland Ranch, CO 80130.

ISBN 13: 978-0-8163-3787-3
ISBN 10: 0-8163-3787-X

13 14 15 16 17 • 5 4 3 2 1

DEDICATION

There is something uniquely special about working with a former student. Indeed, I must hasten to admit that during years past, when looking out over a classroom of energetic idea-generating students, wondering which of them might someday turn out my boss was the furthest thing from my mind! One reason why this is so unexpected is that all through the years, I fully expected to remain in the classroom until the end of my career. But God, in His great wisdom, planned a different scenario, and thus it is that I hereby dedicate the ninth book in The Good Lord Made Them All animal series to my long-ago English student at Southwestern Adventist University who is now the esteemed vice president of Product Development—and such a joy he is to work with!—at Pacific Press® Publishing Association:

JERRY D. THOMAS

CONTENTS

INTRODUCTION

STRANGE AND WONDERFUL

Joseph Leininger Wheeler

As always, when choosing a theme for a book, I sought divine wisdom, for my own wisdom wells are so shallow. In this case, What should my theme be for our ninth animal story collection? After Dogs, Cats, Horses, Wild Animals, Animal Heroes, Small Animals, Animals of the North, and Animals of the Jungle, should I return to an earlier theme, or should I seek out another?

The process proved more than a little frustrating in that the answer was mighty slow in coming. I read, or reread, hundreds of animal stories before a pattern emerged. As I slogged through this long process of discarding one theme after another, I couldn't help but think of that fiendish highwayman of Attica in ancient Greece—Procrustes—who placed all those unfortunates who fell into his hands upon an iron bed. If they were longer than the bed, he cut off whatever lopped over; if they were shorter, he used a rack to stretch them out until they fit. He was eventually slain by Theseus. Hence the term "procrustean bed," which has come to mean "a rigid standard to which conformity is enforced."

Well, at times during this search for a ninth theme, I felt like I was using a procrustean bed to measure each thematic applicant.

But finally, my "Eureka moment": the animal stories I would feature would qualify for inclusion by whether or not each one was sufficiently "strange" or "wonderful." From that moment on, putting this collection together became exciting—exciting because it was such a new and unorthodox theme for a story anthology. It was amazing how elastic those two words turned out to be. A number of stories qualified on both counts.

At first I worried I wouldn't find enough strong stories to qualify; later, I worried because I ended up having to leave a number of them out because there wasn't room for them all—which ones would lose out on my editorial procrustean bed? I consoled myself by reasoning, *Perhaps later on I could put together another collection of strange and wonderful animal stories.*

A number were written by contemporary writers (one completed only hours away from my submission deadline); others were spread out across a span of a century and a half—several appear to be even older than that.

I learned a lot—more than for any other previous collection—I hadn't known before. Some were so improbable that if I hadn't trusted the source I'd have doubted their validity. A very few were apparently fictional; however, I've learned that no writer ever writes in a vacuum: in a majority of cases an ostensibly fictional story is based on an actual occurrence. In fact, the reverse is often true: it is an axiom among writers that the more unlikely to be true a given story appears to be, the more likely it is to be true, for writers of fiction rarely incorporate narratives that deviate too far from verisimilitude—unless they are dealing with pure fantasy.

At any rate, the ball is now in your court. Do write me telling me what you think of the collection, which stores you like best, and why. I can be reached at P.O. Box 1246, Conifer, CO 80433. Or if you prefer, my e-mail is mountainauthor@gmail.com.

* * * * *

Squeaker, the Truck-Riding Deer

Steve Hamilton

In this journey we call "life," once in every long while there comes an experience so incredible that it remains in conscious memory throughout life. Such a story is this, penned by my cousin Steve Hamilton, about our mutual grandparents Rollo and Ruby Wheeler and—well, I'll just let Steve tell this most improbable of all improbable stories.

* * * * *

One of my earliest memories has to do with the summer of 1940 when I was two. Grandpa and Grandma had moved to Howell Mountain overlooking California's Pope Valley and Napa Valley, where their six-hundred-acre ranch seemed to stretch away to forever, at least to me. In those simpler days of the Great Depression, those who had money used it; those who did not, bartered. My grandfather Rollo Wheeler had a big batch of kids who needed a college education; Pacific Union College in Angwin had a voracious boiler heating system that gobbled up a vast supply of wood. Since wood was something Grandpa had plenty of, he and the college met each other's needs. And since one of his daughters, Ruby, married my father, Jay, I got to be there too.

When Dad worked in the woods, I couldn't go out with him because I was barely two years old and it was far too dangerous, but when Grandpa went too, I got to go because he could watch out for me.

One unforgettable day, we arrived on the scene just as the men were putting the finishing touches on felling a huge bull pine tree about ninety feet in height. They'd already finished the undercut and were starting to cut the other side and insert the wedges guiding it to the exact place they wanted it to fall. They'd cleared the brush from the small knoll that they had targeted. But just as it started to fall, a giant whirlwind swirled out of nowhere and engulfed the tree, turning it about forty-five degrees to the right so that it missed the knoll altogether. It came crashing down with a thunderous sound and rolled down into a nearby ravine.

Miraculously, no one was hurt or killed—that was the good news. But the bad news was that they now had to cut the fallen tree into smaller logs and winch them up the steep bank, and this was going to cost them many hours of extra work.

The men all scrambled down the bank to inspect the tree and determine just what to do. Suddenly, they heard moaning and a high-pitched squeaky voice coming from under the downed tree. As it happened, a tragedy had occurred. Unbeknownst to them, a momma white-tailed deer had been giving birth to twin fawns down in what she thought was the protected willows and brush of the little creek running down the ravine. Sadly, a huge limb from that tree had fallen directly on her, killing her and one of the fawns.

Queenie, Grandpa's ten-year-old German Shepherd dog was on the scene in an instant! Grandpa and the boys had to call her off. One of the twin fawns had survived, and it appeared to have been born only minutes before. It still had blood-filled film and afterbirth all over it. Its head and nostrils were clear, however. My dad carried the fawn up to the truck (about two-hundred feet) and gently laid it down. Queenie was there immediately, and Grandpa was certain we'd have a hard time keeping her from injuring or killing the newborn.

Queenie was trained to chase deer and keep them out of Grandpa's twenty-six-acre apple orchard down by the ranch house, and occasionally she had injured and even killed deer that wouldn't immediately leave the orchard. The orchard was fenced on three sides away from the house and it was Queenie's job every night to keep all of the deer out, because a herd of forty or fifty deer could eat Grandpa's entire crop of apples in only a few hours, thus putting him out of business.

Grandpa didn't know what to do. He wanted to save the deer, but it would be impossible for him to keep Queenie away from it. While the men were talking it over, the little fawn started making its funny little squeaking sound, and from then on she was called Squeaker.

The fawn only weighed three or four pounds, and when no one noticed, Queenie quickly stepped over to it and started very gently, and almost affectionately, to lick the afterbirth from the baby.

Part of the story that has not been told was that Queenie had just delivered a litter of seven or eight puppies a day and a half earlier, but they were stillborn, dying during the birthing process. As tragic as that was, because she was ten years old (about seventy years old in human years), stillbirths are not all that unusual for dogs her age.

God has a wonderful way of providing. Queenie's nipples were bulging with milk, and our new baby fawn badly needed nourishment.

Everyone stood back and let Momma Queenie clean and nuzzle the newborn. We all watched in amazement for several minutes. After the men all went back to work, Grandpa helped Queenie to lie down and showed me how to gently squeeze her nipples to get drops of milk and feed them to Squeaker.

The truck gave us shadow from the warm afternoon sun, and I actually taught Squeaker how to nurse, just a little, and within a couple of hours two or three of Queenie's breasts were partially emptying.

My grandpa Rollo was absolutely amazed at how Squeaker took to Queenie. After all, the fawn was only hours, maybe even minutes, old when the tree fell; but after all, this was the only momma she knew, and her doggie momma had the much-needed milk. Queenie was an old dog, set in her ways and trained to dislike and maybe even kill deer; yet here she was falling in motherly love with her new strange-looking baby.

Even though Squeaker was small, she did have long legs, and by the time the afternoon was over, she was trying to stand and nurse her new momma. I was only a two-year-old boy

and couldn't figure how to make this awkward situation work. Momma Dog would lie down very cooperatively and when the fawn would lean over far enough, she would fall face down on top of Momma.

Grandpa arrived on the scene and with him was a large bale of barley straw in the back of the truck. Down came the straw and up came Momma, lying on the straw bale, and *voilà*! Squeaker was at the perfect height to nurse!

When we arrived back at the house, dog and deer were already bonding as momma and baby. My mom and Grandma both were amazed. No one in our households could even imagine such a thing taking place. Because I was only two and had been working at it all afternoon, I didn't think it was such a big deal, but Grandpa and my dad made me feel like I was a hero. Of course, I gladly accepted that status.

Squeaker got Queenie's pen and dog house, and Grandpa made the dog a new home out of bales of barley straw.

Grandpa always got up by 5:30 A.M., and on the nights I stayed with my grandparents, I got up too. Being the nursemaid was my special job, and Grandpa made me feel very important.

When Queenie was not available, Grandma fixed Squeaker some of my own powdered baby formula, and I fed Squeaker from a bottle. She did not like it nearly as well as her adopted momma's milk, though Grandpa solved that problem by taking me, Queenie, and Squeaker with him in the old Model A Ford everywhere he went. That way when Squeaker was hungry, we stopped, and down came the hay bale out of the rumble seat, and we waited until mealtime was over, then we resumed the journey.

I never thought much about it, but we did make a memorable sight. We drove down the road in a Model A Ford with Queenie sitting by the door on the passenger's seat with her head always out the window. A two-and-a-half-going-on-three-year-old Steve was sitting on the same seat but next to the gearshift toward Grandpa. Next, was Squeaker from her little space behind the seats, with her head and nose over Grandpa's shoulder, nuzzling Grandpa's ear. Then, of course, there sat Grandpa, proudly driving us down the road. We did really make a sight to behold when we were in Angwin or St. Helena. People everywhere wanted a peek, and Grandpa kindly consented, provided they kept their distance. Everyone wanted to know how the dog and deer got along so well. My grandpa would smile and say, "Queenie is Squeaker's momma." They all laughed in disbelief and Grandpa never explained as we drove on about our business. Most of the time we were delivering a few boxes of apples off the hay bale in the back to his regular apple clients.

* * * * *

Squeaker kept her reserve and held herself aloof from all but the very immediate family whom she saw on a daily basis. We had friends who would come to visit, and she'd run up to them, smell their clothes, and nuzzle, leaving little slobbers, but she didn't adopt them as friends.

One day at the creek house in Angwin, wealthy Uncle Worth and Aunt Marge came to visit. It was obviously a very special occasion as he was wearing a brand-new white suit with silk outlines on the pockets and the collar, black-and-white oxford shoes with perforated toes, and she had on a brand-new white dress and black-and-white heels to match. By now, Squeaker was four months old, a good-sized fawn. She still had lots of white spots on her honey-brown colored coat. Our little deer could now almost outrun her doggie Momma, and she could definitely out-jump her. When Uncle Worth and Aunt Marge drove into the yard, the dog and deer came running out to meet them. My dad, seeing how they were dressed to kill, called to Queenie to stop and not to jump up, but Squeaker didn't have such good social behavior. Remember, I said Squeaker liked to nuzzle your clothes and would slobber on them and leave brown spots. Dad hollered to Worth, "Clap your hands and she'll go away!" But Worth, thinking she was so cute, reached down while Dad was hollering, *"Don't pick her up!"* Too late! Laughing in his deep baritone voice, Worth had grabbed her and held her face-to-face in front of him. Her hooves were as sharp as razors and within a few seconds she had pawed his new suit and shredded portions of his coat and pants, ruining his entire ensemble. Dad was shocked! Worth and Marge were devastated, but like I said, Squeaker didn't make friends easily.

From about that time on, Grandpa wisely started keeping our little deer out in the barn up at the apple ranch and away from most people. He didn't want her getting used to any more people because he wanted her to eventually be wild again.

My dad was a teacher now, and we lived about twenty miles from the apple ranch. Because I didn't live with Grandpa Rollo and Grandma Ruby during the week, I usually saw them only after church on the weekends down at the creek house. When I did get to see Squeaker, she was still my buddy. She was so tall now that I could barely get my little arm over her neck, but she loved the little snacks Grandma gave me to feed her. Whether it was an apple slice, some oatmeal flakes, or corn bread, she loved them all.

After six or seven months, Squeaker was weaned from her momma's milk, and although she and Queenie were still buddies, they no longer played or slept together, and Grandpa didn't take Squeaker on his apple-delivery trips anymore. Grandpa and

Grandma made the deer spend more and more time alone out in the barn with the cow.

When she was a yearling and had lost her spots, Grandpa would take Squeaker about three miles away down to a lower forty acres called the Astrican apple orchard. Grandpa owned this place too, but it only had two or three acres of trees—and these were special apples that had fruit by the fourth of July. The apples never did get very sweet, but they were great for applesauce. It was a safe area and far enough away from other ranches so she could get acclimated to being alone with other wild deer.

My family moved to the Hilmar/Turlock area of central California, so we seldom saw Squeaker anymore.

One day when I was four, I was riding with Grandpa when we saw a white-tailed doe that looked to be about two years old. That would have matched her age. When we stopped the truck, she started walking over to us. She hesitated at about fifty feet from us. Grandpa was certain it was Squeaker but didn't want to confuse her by getting reacquainted. Grandma was sad but said she also knew it was best.

* * * * *

Grandpa and Grandma Wheeler's place was absolutely the place to be on Thanksgiving. It was not unusual to have as many as seventy family members in attendance. There were cousins that I didn't even know I was related to, and we had a grand old time. Every third year, Cousin Joe and his folks would come home from Central America, where they were missionaries. We would team up with Cousin Billie, and at those times the woods surrounding Grandpa's were a dangerous place to be. Pirates, Wild West renegades, and overall bad guys secretly watched and plotted against society. But the plots were innocent, and the fun was unsurpassed.

On these Thanksgiving weekends, it was traditional for those of the group who were deer hunters to come up to Grandpa's ranch early in the week and try to fill their deer tags and finish out the season. Those who were successful always hung their deer in one of the apple sheds and dressed them out, wrapping them in sheets to hang in the cool night air. Grandpa didn't mind getting rid of a few more that he did not have to chase out of the orchard every night. The Queen Mother (Queenie) had passed on due to old age, and Grandpa had a new patrol dog named Buster. Buster was a huge dog, about 120 pounds, and he became Grandma's favorite companion. Buster's first job was to keep the deer out of Grandma's flower garden, and his next job was to chase them out of the orchard. He had taken over Queenie's jobs and did them both well.

Buster's allegiance was primarily to Grandma, and Grandpa didn't mind it at all. Grandma needed protection because she'd been deaf since she was twenty-two as the result of complications from diphtheria.

I was ten years old before I heard anyone mention anything more about Squeaker.

After the men would come up and shoot their deer and dress them out, Grandma would let us eat venison for part of Thanksgiving dinner along with some of the best food you could ever imagine. However, after Squeaker had become part of our lives, she'd no longer permit anyone to prepare or cook any deer meat in the house. It had to be barbequed outside.

When she spoke about it to Grandpa, she spoke in a very hoarse whisper. Even though she did not intonate the voice, she whispered so loudly you could hear her clear across the room. She would corner Grandpa in front of all the relatives just before we were to eat and, pointing to the venison, she'd say, "It's Squeaker, isn't it?"

"No, Ma, they were all bucks, no does!"

"Are you sure, Pa? We can't have the blessing and eat if it's Squeaker!"

"No, Ma, I'm positive these were boy deer." Then she would give the OK, and we could bless the food and begin the feast.

Who knew that Squeaker would have such an impact on the Wheeler household, even in absentia and for years after she was back in the wild? I have often thought, *I wonder if she ever mated and raised baby fawns of her own? If so, I wonder how many? I wonder how long she lived? I wonder where she lived? Did she remember us? Did she remember her doggie momma? I guess I'll never know!*

* * * * *

"Squeaker, the Truck-Riding Deer," by Steve Hamilton. Copyright © 2012. Printed by permission of the author. All rights reserved. Steve Hamilton lives and writes from his home in Silver Springs, Nevada.

"I Love You, Pat Myers"

Jo Coudert

Pat Myers was going bonkers alone in her empty house. Anything would be better than oppressing loneliness.
Enter Casey.

* * * * *

"I'm going nuts here by myself," Pat Myers confessed to her daughter, Annie. Pat had been virtually confined to her house for a year as she was treated for an inflamed artery in her temple that affected her vision and stamina.

A widow with two married children, she'd been happily running a chain of dress shops. But now that she had to give up her business, her home began to feel oppressively silent and empty. Finally she admitted to Annie how lonely she was.

"Do you think I should advertise for someone to live with me?"

"That's such a gamble," Annie said. "How about a pet?"

"I haven't the strength to walk a dog," Pat said. "I'm allergic to cats, and fish don't have a whole lot to say."

"Birds do," said her daughter. "Why not get a parrot?" And so it began.

Pat and Annie visited a breeder of African Greys and were shown two little featherless creatures huddled together for warmth. Pat was doubtful, but Annie persuaded her to put a deposit down on the bird with the bright eyes. When he was three months old and feathered out, he was delivered to his new owner, who named him Casey.

A few weeks later, Pat told Annie, "I didn't realize I talked so much. Casey's picking up all kinds of words."

"I told you." Her daughter smiled at the sound of pleasure in Pat's voice.

The first sentence Casey learned was, "Where's my glasses?" followed by, "Where's my purse?" Whenever Pat began scanning tabletops and opening drawers, Casey chanted, "Where's my glasses? Where's my purse?" When she returned from an errand, he'd greet her with, "Holy smokes, it's cold out there," in a perfect imitation of her voice.

Casey disliked being caged, so Pat often let him roam the house. "What fun it is to have him," she told Annie. "It makes the whole place feel better."

"I think you're beginning to feel better too," said Annie.

"Well, he gives me four or five laughs a day—they say laughter's good for a person."

Once a plumber came to repair a leak under the kitchen sink. In the den, Casey cracked seeds in his cage and eyed the plumber through the open door. Suddenly, the parrot broke the silence, reciting, "One potato, two potato, three potato, four...."

"What?" asked the plumber.

"Don't poo on the rug," Casey ordered, in Pat's voice.

The plumber pushed himself out from under the sink and marched to the living room. "If you're going to play games, lady, you can just get yourself another plumber." Pat looked at him blankly. The plumber hesitated. "That was *you*, wasn't it?"

Pat smiled. "*What* was me?"

"One potato, two potato—and don't poo on the rug."

"Oh, dear!" said Pat. "Let me introduce you to Casey."

Casey saw them coming. "What's going on around here?" he said.

At that moment, Pat sneezed. Casey immediately mimicked the sneeze, added a couple of Pat's coughs at her allergic worst and finished with Pat's version of "Wow!" The plumber shook his head slowly and crawled back under the sink.

One morning while Pat was reading the paper, the phone rang. She picked it up and got a dial tone. The next morning it rang again, and again she got a dial tone. The third morning she realized what was going on: Casey had learned to mimic the phone faultlessly.

Once, as Pat opened a soda can at the kitchen table, Casey waddled over and snatched at the can. It toppled, sending a cascade of cola onto her lap and the floor. "*#@!" Pat said. Casey eyed her. "Forget you heard that," she ordered. "I didn't say it. I never say it. And I wouldn't have now if I hadn't just mopped the floor." Casey kept his beak shut.

Later a real estate agent arrived to go over some business. She and Pat were deep in discussion when Casey screamed from the den, "*#@!"

Both women acted as though they'd heard nothing.

Liking the sibilance, Casey tried it again. "*#@!" he said. And again, "*#@!, *#@! *#@!"

Caught between humiliation and amusement, Pat put her hand on her guest's arm. "Helen, it's sweet of you to pretend, but I know you haven't suddenly gone deaf." They both broke up laughing.

"Oh, you bad bird," Pat scolded after the agent left. "She's going to think I go around all day saying four-letter words."

"What a mess," Casey said.

"You're right," Pat told him.

Casey's favorite perch in the kitchen was the faucet in the sink; his favorite occupation, trying to remove the washer at the end of it. Once, to tease him, Pat sprinkled a handful of water over him. Casey ceased his attack on the washer and swiveled his head to look at her sharply. "What's the matter with you?" he demanded.

If he left the kitchen and Pat heard him say, "Oh, you bad bird!" she knew to come running. Casey was either pecking at her dining room chairs or the wallpaper in the foyer.

"Is it worth it?" her son, Bill, asked, looking at the damaged front hall.

"Give me a choice between a perfect, lonely house and a tacky, happy one," said Pat, "and I'll take the tacky one any day."

But Pat did decide to have Casey's sharp claws clipped. To trim them without getting bitten, the vet wrapped Casey tightly in a towel, turned him on his back and handed him to an assistant to hold while he went to work. A helpless Casey looked at Pat and said piteously, "Oh, the poor baby."

Pat often wondered if Casey knew what he was saying. Sometimes the statements were so appropriate she couldn't be sure. Like the time a guest had lingered on and on talking in the doorway and Casey finally called out impatiently, "Night, night."

Yet, whenever Pat wanted to teach him something, Casey could be maddening. Once she carried him to the living room and settled in an easy chair as Casey sidled up her arm and nestled his head against her chest. Pat dusted the tips of her fingers over his velvet-gray feathers and scarlet tail. "I love you," she said. "Can you say, 'I love you, Pat Myers'?"

Casey cocked an eye at her. "I live on Mallard View," he said.

"I know where you live, funny bird. Tell me you love me."

"Funny bird."

Another time Pat was trying to teach Casey "Jingle Bell Rock" before her children and grandchildren arrived for Christmas dinner. "It'll be your contribution," she told him.

"Where's my glasses?"

"Never mind that. Just listen to me sing." But as Pat sang, "Jingle bell, jingle bell, jingle bell rock," and danced around the kitchen, Casey simply looked at her.

Finally Pat gave up. And all through Christmas dinner Casey was silent. When it came time for dessert, Pat extinguished the lights and touched a match to the plum pudding. As the brandy blazed up, with impeccable timing Casey burst into "Jingle bell, jingle bell, jingle bell rock!"

Pat's health improved so much she decided to go on a three-week vacation. "You'll be all right," she told Casey. "You can stay with Annie and the kids."

The day her mother was due back, Annie returned Casey to the apartment so he'd be there when Pat got home from the airport.

"Hi, Casey!" Pat called as she unlocked the door. There was no answer. "Holy smokes, it's cold out there!" she said. More silence. Pat dropped her coat and hurried into the den. Casey glared at her.

"Hey, aren't you glad to see me?" The bird moved to the far side of the cage. "Come on, don't be angry," Pat said. She opened the door of the cage and held out her hand. Casey dropped to the bottom of the cage and huddled there.

In the morning Pat tried again. Casey refused to speak. Later that day he consented to climb onto her wrist and be carried to the living room. When she sat down, he shifted uneasily and seemed about to fly away. "Please, Casey," Pat pleaded. "I know I was away a long time, but you've got to forgive me."

Casey took a few tentative steps up her arm, then moved back to her knee. "Were you afraid I was never going to come back?" she said softly. "I would never do that."

Casey cocked his head and slowly moved up her arm. Pat crooked her elbow, and Casey nestled against her. Pat stroked his head, smoothing his feathers with her forefinger. Finally Casey spoke.

"I love you, Pat Myers," he said.

* * * * *

" 'I Love You, Pat Myers,' " by Jo Coudert. Printed by permission of the author. Jo Coudert, a well-known professional writer, lives and writes from her home in Califon, New Jersey.

"If God Gives You a Cat, I'll Let You Keep It"

Hank Arends

A Las Vegas oddsmaker wouldn't touch this story!

* * * * *

We have heard the old expression of raining cats and dogs—especially in Oregon—but this is ridiculous.

The story—maintained to be true—tells of the pastor who had a kitten that refused to come down from a tree in his backyard.

The newsletter of St. Paul's Episcopal Church in Salem related what came next: "The pastor coaxed and coaxed it, offering it warm milk, treats, etc., but the kitten would not budge."

Then, like Ford, the pastor had a better idea. Because the tree was too frail to climb, he tied a rope from the tree to his car. The idea was that he would gradually bend the tree down until he could retrieve the kitten.

"He kept checking his progress in the car frequently; the tree was bending nicely. He thought if he went just a little farther, the tree would be bent sufficiently for him to reach the kitten."

"But as he moved the car ahead, the rope broke . . . *twang!* . . . and the kitten instantly sailed through the air . . . out of sight! The pastor felt terrible."

A canvass of the neighborhood failed to reveal anyone who had seen an airborne kitten. As he headed home, the pastor prayed, "Lord, I just commit this kitten to your keeping."

A few days later, the pastor met a known cat-hating member of his congregation buying cat food at the grocery store. He asked her about the purchase.

"You won't believe this," was her response.

She told of her little daughter begging and begging for a cat and being refused again and again.

The weary mother finally said, "Well, if God gives you a cat, I'll let you keep it."

The little girl went outside, knelt, and prayed to God for a cat.

"Pastor," the lady said, "you won't believe this, but I saw it with my own eyes. A kitten suddenly came flying out of the blue sky with its paws outspread and landed right in front of her."

The moral of the story? Never underestimate the power of God.

* * * * *

"'If God Gives You a Cat, I'll Let You Keep It,'" by Hank Arends. Copyright © by Statesman Journal. Reprinted by permission. Hank Arends lives and writes from his home in the Northwest.

JIM AND THE GIANT

Helen Ward Banks

Jim was lonely, for Cynthia left him alone every day while she went out to slay what she called "dragons." Cynthia called him her little hero, but he didn't feel like one. Then, one never-to-be-forgotten day, Jim heard a squeak.

* * * * *

"Are you going to be too lonely, little brother?"

"It's pretty lonely, Sinsie," Jim answered.

"Everybody's lonely at times, I guess," sighed Cynthia. "Some day you'll be grown up, won't you? Then you'll go out and fight the dragons, and I'll be just your lonely little sister staying home to keep the castle."

"Couldn't you take me with you, Sinsie?" begged Jim.

She laughed, pulling on her glove, and stooped to kiss him.

"I'd have to carry you shut up in my handbag all day, and how that would squeeze your legs! Guard the castle well, Jimmy boy. I'll bring back something wonderful for supper. Today's payday, you know."

"I wish the masons hadn't finished building the wall," Jim grieved. "It was fun talking to them."

Cynthia sighed and smiled—like an April shower with the sun chasing it.

"I know how it feels to be lonely, little brother, but we can't stop to think about it. Remember, our grandfather fought with Robert Lee, and we have to be heroes, don't we? If I didn't go out to fight the dragons, we'd starve together in the castle, and that would be very disagreeable."

"It's a funny castle," smiled Jim—"just a little bit of a wooden house. I wish Greatheart would come and take us out."

"There isn't any Greatheart," said Cynthia, her lips very straight. "Once I thought there was, but there isn't. There's just you and me, Jimmy boy, forever. And you're a hero; you're brave enough to stay alone, aren't you?"

"Yes, Sinsie," answered Jim, his head tilting like Cynthia's.

Cynthia kissed him again and held him tight for an instant. "That's my brave little soldier! It's such a lovely day after last night's storm that you can be out all day; and your milk for lunch is in the pantry. You'll be all right, won't you?"

Jim nodded. "But I wish I had something to talk to."

Cynthia stopped by the table that held Jim's books. "Why here are lots of friends to talk to! See, here's the *Elephant Child;* let's stand him on the sofa. And here's *Brer Rabbit;* he can sit here on the table. And here's old Christian going out to meet the lions; where shall we put him?"

"Don't open *Pilgrim's Progress,*" Jim interposed hastily. "Giant Despair might come out, and he's *awful.*"

For an instant quick tears brimmed Cynthia's eyes, but she laughed them away— laughter was the only weapon she held against that same old giant.

"Giant Despair is nothing but a bogey, Jim. Just whack him hard, and you find he isn't there. I hate to leave you, buddie, but I can't feed you and stay with you too."

"Maybe sometime we'll be rich enough to live in a real castle," said Jim, "and then you can stay with me all the time."

"If dollars would only count up a little faster," sighed Cynthia.

"Never mind," comforted Jim. "We'll play this is a castle, and that's just as good. And you love me better than anything else in all the world, don't you, Sinsie?"

"Better than anyone in the world," she answered with a little catch in her voice. "Now, kiss me once more and let me fly. And you and Brer Rabbit and the Elephant Child with his 'satiable curiosity' guess all day what I'm going to bring for supper. Goodbye, dearest boy."

"Goodbye," said Jim with his bravest smile. He was still smiling it when Cynthia turned at the curve for a farewell wave, but as she went out of sight it dropped.

Those masons were nice, he thought. *I like talking friends better than just pictures. I wish I had a kitten—'cept Sinsie doesn't like cats much. Kittens can't talk, but they're alive.*

Jim sat down on the top step of the porch and looked at the cobblestone wall with which the friendly masons had encircled the meadow across the road. Only yesterday they had been there, but last night they had loaded all their wonder-working pails and boards and trowels into a truck and driven off out of Jim's life. Now there was just the long line of wall opposite, the pale, Indian-summer sky above, and the yellow leaves dropping softly down to the brown earth beneath, not another sight nor another sound. It *was* lonely.

But as Jim sat and gazed at the cobblestone wall across the road, suddenly he chuckled.

"I see Brer Rabbit built into the wall over there," he said. "I bet old Mike made him; Mike's such a joker. He's made out of a big stone like an egg, and he's got two long, flat stones for ears, and he's sitting up on his hind legs. Hello, Brer Rabbit!"

And it almost seemed as if Brer Rabbit squeaked a response.

Then, laughing aloud, Jim came to his feet. "And down there by the corner is the

Elephant Child before the crocodile pulled his nose long; his ears are long, though. I'll bet Mike made that too. Hello, Elephant Child!"

Did the Elephant Child also squeak a faint "Hello"?

"They're nice," breathed Jim, "almost as nice as alive." Then his eyes traveled in the other direction. He drew a short breath, and a frown drove away his smile as he took a backward step toward the open door.

"It's that old Giant Despair!" he declared. "Mike didn't make him. I wonder how he got built into that wall! He's got pop eyes and a big, flat nose and a huge, big mouth wide open. He looks just like his picture. He's horrid. I won't stay out here."

He went into the house and closed the door. The *Elephant Child* still sat on the sofa between his green covers, and *Brer Rabbit* perched on the table with no covers at all. In spite of their company, Jim realized that he was only eight years old and that he had a long, sisterless day ahead of him.

He sat down on the sofa beside the *Elephant Child,* keeping his back to the window. But he could not help now and then casting a glance over his shoulder to see if Giant Despair had gone away. He was always still there, sitting on the stone wall, and Jim each time hastily turned his back.

"I'm afraid," he whispered. But he couldn't help turning to look again. Then he pulled down the shades, and presently he locked the door. As a final act of oblivion, he carried his red *Pilgrim's Progress* up to his own cupboard, where he hid it under a pillow and buttoned the cupboard door.

"Now he can't get me," he declared as he came downstairs.

But on the bottom stair Jim faltered. It was all right for him, but how about the Elephant Child and Brer Rabbit built into that same fence with Giant Despair, unable to escape? They were Jim's friends, and men stood by their friends, especially heroes did whose grandfather had fought under Lee. Sinsie said Jim was a hero. Sinsie said, too, that if you whacked Giant Despair hard enough, he couldn't hurt you.

With a pale face and thumping heart, Jim went back to his room for his wooden sword and stamped down again to the outer door. Resolutely he unlocked it and, brandishing his sword hero-wise, marched down the steps, across the grass, and across the road. Then he heard a sound. It was Giant Despair squeaking at him. Jim's hero blood paled to water; he turned his back on his foe, and the next instant he was scrambling up the porch steps.

"He squeaked at me," Jim gasped as he banged the door behind him. "He did squeak."

He tumbled down on the sofa with his pounding heart, very frightened and very ashamed.

"I ran," he accused himself. "Heroes don't run. I ran before I gave Giant Despair one whack. I've got to go back and whack him whether he squeaks or not."

He made three attempts before he got once more through the door and across the road, forcing his quaking legs to their best soldier stride. He advanced on Giant Despair with uplifted sword, strengthening his fluttering heart for the "whack" that was to slay his foe. Then the giant squeaked again.

Jim stopped with a gasp. But now his legs obeyed his hero will and stood. It was only a moment's halt before Jim charged his foe and, shutting his eyes tight, dealt a doughty blow at Giant Despair's ugly head.

For an instant Jim stood with closed eyes and quick breath awaiting reprisals. But nothing happened. He opened his eyes a crack and peeped. There lay the impassive stone wall as it had lain before he struck.

Suddenly Jim laughed aloud. If he had not dislodged Giant Despair, he had slain his own fear. Sinsie was right. If you whacked Giant Despair hard enough, you found he wasn't there.

"Hun," scoffed Jim; "I thought you were Giant Despair, and you're only an old stone wall. You couldn't even squeak."

But something squeaked: it did it again over in the meadow. Jim heard, but his blow had turned his fear to daring.

"You're only an old stone wall," he repeated, "and I'm going to climb over you. I'm going over to those trees to see what's squeaking."

He stuck an exploring foot into a cobblestone crevice, seized with a bold hand Giant Despair's nose, and by that help scaled the wall and dropped down into the meadow on the other side, where, with the courage of a Drake, he laid his course through the stubbly sea to the island of trees in the middle. No weak knees now, nor hanging hands, but an upflung head and a heart burning with the spirit of adventure and discovery.

And he did discover something on his desert island—a little white, rough-coated dog with brown spots over his pleading brown eyes, and a piteous little *squeak,* and a tail that wagged when he saw Jim. His dragging chain had caught around a sapling, and it held him prisoner. He licked Jim's face when Jim dropped his sword and went down on his knees with freeing intent.

"You love me," Jim quivered, his arms around the little beast, "and I love you. I've discovered you; you're mine. You'll live with me forever and ever, and I'll never be lonely anymore, even when Sinsie's gone. I'll name you Rover. You're sopping wet, Rover. You've been out in the storm all night. And I bet you're hungry. Somebody didn't take very good care of you. I'll give you half my milk. I'm glad I found you."

The puppy licked Jim's face again, shook himself, and was ready to follow Jim to the end of the world.

"I don't know how I'll get you over the wall," doubted Jim, chain in one hand and sword in the other.

But the dog did that for himself with a leap up and a leap down that tumbled Jim, at the end of the chain, into the road faster than he meant to go. As he picked himself up, old Giant Despair seemed to give him a friendly wink with a pop eye.

"Maybe you're a good giant, after all," said Jim. "Maybe that's what whacking does to you. Maybe you were trying to tell me about Rover. I'm much obliged to you, for I'm very happy."

In the warm, bright little kitchen Rover disposed of his half of Jim's milk with a few curls of his red tongue and confidingly wagged for more.

"You're *awful* hungry," Jim said, and raided the pantry again. "I'll just have to give you this beefsteak bone, even if Sinsie was going to make hash of its meat."

The beefsteak bone and a slice or two of bread seemed to fill even the puppy's empty stomach. His wet coat Jim rubbed dry with a convenient dish towel. Then the two young things frolicked together until the puppy, reminiscent of his long, rainy vigil, decided a nap was in order and flopped down beside the stove. Jim dropped beside him, an arm over the dog, and in the quiet comfort of companionship, he also fell asleep.

It was midafternoon when Jim awoke and sat up. The terrier opened his eyes, stretched his legs, flapped his stub tail once, and slept off again.

"You must be awful tired," said Jim. "I wish you wanted to come for a walk."

But the puppy didn't.

"All right, you can get rested," said Jim, " 'cause you're mine now, and we can play every day forever. It isn't lonely anymore. Sinsie'll come soon now, and I'll tell her all about you. I guess I'll go and meet her."

He shut Rover carefully into the kitchen and padded away down the lane that led to the post-road. That was forbidden ground, but he climbed a stone wall at the corner and sat smiling and kicking his feet as he waited for Cynthia's trolley to bring her home.

Most of the passersby smiled at the gallant little figure and a few spoke to him. But no one stopped until a man with more somberness in his dark eyes than his youth called for glanced at him, looked again as he passed, stopped, went on, and finally turned back to speak.

"Do you belong here?" he asked.

"No," smiled Jim. "I live down the lane. I'm looking for Sinsie. I've waited most an hour, I guess."

"I'm looking for someone too," said the man, "and it's taken me hundreds of hours even to get on her track. May I sit on the wall by you for a while?"

Jim made cordial room. "Sinsie's my sister," he explained. "She goes to the city and fights dragons, and I stay home and keep the castle. It isn't really a castle, you know, or real dragons, but we play it is. It's fun living with Sinsie, for she always plays. First I lived with my uncle, while Sinsie was going to college, but I don't anymore. Who do you live with?"

"With no one. I did have a dog, but even he broke his chain last night and ran away from me."

Jim gave an uneasy start. "I guess your dog was black, wasn't he?" he inquired.

"No, white; a rough-haired terrier named Nailer."

"I guess he didn't have any spots on him?" asked anxious Jim.

"One over each eye."

"I guess they were—were pink spots?" ventured Jim once more.

"Brown."

"Oh!" said Jim, and relapsed into despondency. Grown-ups ruled the world. Just as soon as a little boy found a dog, a big man could come and take it away. Then Jim straightened under an unconscious thought. His dog was Rover, shut safely in the kitchen, and, if Jim didn't tell, how could the man find out whether Rover looked like Nailer? Under the inspiration of that thought, Jim started conversation again.

"It's a very nice day," he observed.

"It's a bully day," assented the man, rousing from his abstraction; "and I think you're a fine chap too. Don't you want to tell me your name?"

"Jim," the child answered. If this man hadn't lost a dog, he really would be quite a pleasant companion. "What's yours?"

"Mine is Dan."

"Isn't that funny!" cried Jim. "Dan is Sinsie's favorite name. What is your favorite name?"

"Cynthia," said Dan, watching Jim's face.

"Why, that's awful funny! That's Sinsie's name."

Dan drew a deep breath. "I thought I couldn't mistake the eyes. So you're the little brother!"

"I'm all Sinsie's got, and Sinsie's all I've got," agreed Jim. "She loves me better than anyone in the world and I love her better than anyone in the world."

"I can believe that."

"I get awful lonely when Sinsie goes away all day. But I like to live with her. Do you ever get lonely?"

"Lonely as hell."

"Sinsie won't let me say that word," breathed Jim. "That must be awful lonely. Sinsie's lonely too; she said so; but I don't believe she's as lonely as—hell. She's got me, you see. I saw a picture of hell once in a big Bible. It was worse than Giant Despair even. Do you know Giant Despair?"

"He lives with me."

"Does he?" whispered Jim. "Why don't you run away?"

"I did. I got clear away and came as far as this. But Giant Despair gripped me again, and he's held me tight ever since I've been here."

Jim peered around at the wall beyond his new friend. "He doesn't show," he whispered.

"You won't know what he looks like for a good many years yet."

"I do know what he looks like," protested Jim. "He's in my *Pilgrim's Progress*, and he's ugly. I locked *Pilgrim's Progress* in my cupboard, and then I saw Giant Despair out on the stone wall."

"It's a way he has of turning up. Did he frighten you?"

Jim nodded. "I ran," he confided in a low little voice.

Dan laughed shortly. "Friends in misery, eh? I'm running now."

"But you don't have to," broke in Jim eagerly. "Sinsie said if you whack Giant Despair good and hard, you'll find he isn't there. And when I saw Giant Despair built into the fence, first I ran away, but then I remembered what Sinsie said about his not being there if you whacked. And I did. And he wasn't. He just turned into a good giant and showed me a little dog—b-b-lack with b-b-lue spots," he added hastily.

Dan grinned unwillingly. "That's a new breed."

"He's a very nice dog," went on Jim severely. "His name's Rover. And the person he belonged to before couldn't have tooken very good care of him. I found him out in the field all catched up in some trees with his chain, and he was awful wet and *awful* hungry. I dried him on a dish towel and gave him half my milk and all of Sinsie's best beefsteak bone, and he's mine. I'm going to keep him forever. He loves me. He wants to stay with me."

"All right," agreed Dan, his eyes somber again. "When one's living hand in hand with Giant Despair, I suppose a dog more or less doesn't count."

Jim slipped a comradely hand into Dan's. "If you're afraid of Giant Despair, I'll hold your hand while you hit him."

Dan held the hand tight and looked down at the child. "You're a good pal, aren't you. But, you see—there's a girl. She has blue eyes like yours. They used to be just as frank and warm and gay as yours. I came away up here to see her, for I thought if I saw her I could make things all right. But when I got here, I got cold feet. I've hung around three days, and just half an hour ago I made up my mind to give up and go back to town. Giant Despair told me I had to go. He told me that girl's eyes would be frozen blue ice and I daren't face them."

"But whack him!" cried Jim vehemently, withdrawing his hand to illustrate the action. "If you hit him like that, he'll run. I tell you he will."

"I'm a coward, Jim, a quitter."

"I was, too, first, so we're something alike," confessed Jim; "but I couldn't really be one because my grandfather fought under Robert Lee. Did yours?"

"Mine fought under Ulysses S. Grant."

"He's a good general too," approved Jim kindly. "You can't be a coward if you had a soldier grandfather. You're a hero."

"Not much hero about me," answered Dan with his short, bitter laugh, and then he sat still and looked at nothing again.

Jim kicked his heels against the wall, cast furtive glances at his companion, till at last he could stand it no longer.

"If you're always as lonely as—as—hell, you can have the dog," he volunteered. "His spots aren't bright blue, they're sort of a brownish blue; and he's sort of whitish black."

"You're true blue if the dog isn't," said Dan with that same unwilling grin. Then he sobered. "You're a gentleman, Jim, from the word go. You make me feel as if I'd like to tell you the story, man to man. I haven't had anyone to talk to but Nailer, you see."

"I love stories," smiled Jim, hitching nearer. "Sinsie tells bully ones."

"This isn't a nice story," said Dan grimly, "but I'd like to get it off my chest, and you won't know what I'm talking about enough to hurt you. It's a story about a man who was a beast."

"I love beasts," smiled Jim again.

"Not this kind. The man cared for a girl more than anyone in the world and the girl cared for him. But there was a little brother, a chap like you, and an uncle who wanted to adopt him and leave the girl free, but the girl said she'd never marry the man unless he'd take the little chap, too, and the man—who had never seen the little brother—said why not let the uncle have him. And the girl flared up—mad, you know—and said, all right, then, she'd take care of the boy herself, and the man, who was a beast, told her that if she cared more for the kid than she did for him—all right! And he was mad, too, and went away and stayed away a long time sulking, till when he went back at last to say he was sorry, the girl was gone. It was months before he could trace her, and all that time he lived in hell, hand in hand with Giant Despair. Then he found out where she lived and went hot-foot after her to tell her he couldn't do without her, but old Giant Despair got there first and told the man he was a fool, for the girl would never forgive him. The man tried for three days to swat the giant and see the girl, but the giant stood in his path every time and turned him back, till the man was just going to the hotel for his luggage to go back to town and give it all up, when he saw a little chap with blue eyes sitting on a stone wall—"

"And there sat the little brother," cut in Jim, forgetting personalities in his child's belief of having stories fit. "And then what happened?"

"I don't know anymore. It's up to you now."

"Then," romanced Jim, "the man said, 'How are you, my little friend?'; and the boy said, 'Very well'; and the man said, 'I have a very nice dog I'd like to give you'; and the boy said, 'Thank you'; and then he told his sister, 'This man is my friend; he gave me a very nice dog, and he's sorry he was cross to you. I love him, and will you please love him too?' and, because she always did what her little brother asked her to, she did. And she married the man and lived happy ever after—and the little brother—and the dog. Does that end right?"

Somewhere back inside Dan's eyes there sprang suddenly a flash of light. "By Jove!" he exclaimed. "It's perfectly bully. It takes the little brother to tell the story as well as to kill the giant. I never thought that he could end the story. Is that straight? Do sisters do what their little brothers ask them to?"

"Sinsie always does—when I coax."

"By Jove!" repeated Dan. "You're a pretty little chap to carry a man into the kingdom of heaven on your shoulders. But we are pals, aren't we? You see, I never knew you before. And are you sure about that old giant?"

"Try and see," replied Jim succinctly.

Dan laughed—a laugh as free and gay as Jim's now—and came to his feet. "I will. Let's go and see that pale black dog. If it's mine, I'm going to give it to you. I owe you that for telling me about Giant Despair and ending the story for me."

Jim, too, slipped to the ground and stood looking anxiously at the man. "Won't you be as lonely—as—"

"Never again, little pal, if your story is true," laughed Dan. "Shake! Now we're friends for sure, and Nailer shall nail the bargain. Let's go and see him—and the castle. I think you'd better keep hold of my hand, and then I can't run away if I want to."

"You won't want to run," smiled Jim, hopping along on one foot. "You won't, even when you see Giant Despair built into the fence. I know you're a hero by your eyes."

"The girl said that once," murmured Dan, and then they tramped on together down the lane without a word, but Dan's eyes were not somber anymore.

"There's the house," said Jim, "and there's Giant Despair in the wall; isn't he ugly?"

"Pretty bad!" assented Dan. "But he isn't a patch on the real thing. What must I do to show him I'm going to cut loose? Hit him?"

"You don't have to hit him if you know he's only a stone wall," answered Jim. "Tell him he is and you'll see. I'll hold your hand."

"Giant Despair," declaimed Dan with a wave of the hand that was free, "you are only a stone wall that any donkey can get over. You can't fool me any longer. The Great Wall of China couldn't keep me now from the girl I love."

"You see!" said Jim.

"I see," said Dan.

"Now let's find Nailer. Listen to him squeak! That's what he did this morning, and I thought it was Giant Despair. I'm glad I didn't keep on being a coward or I wouldn't have found Nailer."

"Or I Cynthia! You killed Giant Despair for me as well as for yourself, little pal."

"Couldn't we kill him for Sinsie too?" asked Jim, standing still. "We could. Maybe? Couldn't we?"

"We'll do our best," Dan answered with a straight set to his jaw. "If we can help it, she never shall see him again. I'm going to wait and tell her about it."

Jim, on the top step of the porch, turned with a sudden beaming face. "I've got a bully plan. You have half of Nailer and I'll have half, and then we'll all four live together and nobody will be lonely. Isn't that a good plan?"

"Perfectly bully!" agreed Dan—"If Cynthia likes it."

"She will if I coax her," said Jim confidently. "I'll 'splain it to her as soon as she comes. Just listen to Nailer! I guess he knows you."

"I guess he does. Let's bring him out and I'll show you his tricks."

And that was what Cynthia saw as she came down the lane, smiling to think how Jim would like the plummy buns she had for him. She heard Jim's laugh before she turned the curve of the road. And then she saw. On the lowest porch step Dan sat, one arm flung around Jim in his lap, leaning a golden curly head trustingly against Dan's chest while they watched together a puppy's antics. Cynthia caught her breath, and her eyes grew wide. She knew just how safe a head felt on that resting place.

Then Jim saw her and wriggled to his feet. "There's Sinsie!" he cried. "I'll 'splain about it, Sinsie."

But Dan had risen, too, his brown eyes brimmed with pleading and penitence, fire and love. His arms—emptied of Cynthia's little brother—opened for Cynthia, and, without waiting for any explanation at all, Cynthia walked straight into them.

* * * * *

"Jim and the Giant," by Helen Ward Banks. Published in Scribner's Magazine, *February 1918. Original text owned by Joe Wheeler. Helen Ward Banks was a well-known author of stories and books early in the twentieth century.*

THE SWALLOWS' REVENGE

Margaret Watson

Turns out two swallows could have given Alfred Hitchcock a run for his money!

* * * * *

We are all very fond of the swallows. They go darting about so quickly, make such a pretty little twittering, and never do any harm, only good, because they eat up the flies that nobody wants.

We used to wish and wish that a pair would build a nest in our porch, over the front door, as they did in the porch of Mrs. Nutt's cottage.

We wished and wished—and then one spring morning, when we came in from our walk with Miss Wilson, our governess, Nancy said, "I do believe the swallows are going to build in the porch at last. There's a bit of mud stuck on the wall."

"Oh, where?" we all cried.

"Just there, up under the roof," said Nancy, pointing to it.

Then we all saw it. Just a few little dabs of mud sticking on the wall.

"Do you think the swallows did that?" I asked doubtfully.

And then, while we watched, a swallow came darting in over our heads and put another little dab of mud on the wall.

"There!" cried Nancy. "What do you say to that?"

So we sat and watched the swallows—all but Molly. First one and then the other came flying in and clung to the wall with its claws and wings, while it plastered a bit of mud on the nest.

We spent most of our spare time at that window for the next day or two. It was so jolly to see the nest growing into shape.

The birds twittered over it and talked to each other about it.

At last it was all plastered up, except the hole at which the birds were to go in and out, and they twittered round it, and flew up and down, as though they were looking to see if there was anything else they could do.

But they couldn't see anything, so they darted away to catch a few flies for themselves and rest a little on the telegraph wires.

In the morning, the nest looked all right; but at noon, when we looked at it, there was a straw sticking out!

"What's that for?" I said. "I didn't know swallows lined their nests with straw."

"They don't," said Nancy, looking serious.

"You don't think—" cried Dora, breathlessly.

"I do, though," said Nancy.

"Why, what do you mean, Nancy?" asked Miss Wilson.

"Sparrows build nests with straw."

"Oh!" cried Molly. "Would a sparrow steal a swallow's nest?"

"They do, sometimes," answered Nancy.

"What can we do?" said Dora.

"Couldn't we wait and frighten the sparrows away?" I suggested.

"No use," said Nancy. "That would be impossible, for we can't stay here all day."

"If you wouldn't mind lifting me up, Miss Wilson, I'd take that straw out, anyhow," I said.

So Miss Wilson lifted me up, and I pulled the straw out, and a feather came with it.

But we all felt anxious. Sparrows are not easily discouraged.

* * * * *

We hurried down to the dining-room window as soon as we could; Miss Wilson actually said we might do our practicing in the evening. She was really interested in the stolen nest herself.

So we watched, and very soon a saucy little cock sparrow came, carrying a feather in his mouth, and popped into the nest, and bustled round and round in it, and then came out; and then the hen sparrow came, looking very slim and smooth, and she had a long straw, and dragged it after her into the nest, and twisted it round and round till she got it all in.

But just then the swallows came back.

They flew to their nest with a rush, twittering in a very anxious kind of way; and the hen sparrow put her head out of the hole and ruffled up all her feathers, and the cock ruffled up his feathers and flew at them, pecking right and left. The poor swallows beat about with their wings, gave little harsh cries, and swept about the porch; but the sparrows had the nest, and their beaks were much stronger and harder than the swallows'.

"I'll turn that provoking hen sparrow out, anyway," said Dora.

So she carried a chair into the porch, and climbed upon it, and then the sparrow flew out; and, as soon as she took the chair away, one of the swallows flew in and turned round and round in it, flinging out the feathers and straw, and twittered away as happily as possible.

We were all so pleased.

But next morning, when we came down to breakfast, we found the sparrows had the nest again. So it seemed useless to do anything more.

When we came in before dinner, we saw the swallows hovering about, and heard them talking to each other. So we settled down to watch.

We saw that the cock sparrow was inside the nest, making out to be very busy arranging it, and the hen bird kept bringing him straws and feathers; but both the swallows came up with bits of mud in their beaks.

Suddenly, they darted into the porch, and each put a dab of mud on the mouth of the nest.

The sparrow looked out and pecked at them, but he didn't try to come out; and the hen sparrow went inside too.

Then one swallow flew away, while the other waited, hovering round the nest; and presently the first one flew back with some mud, swooped in, and put it on the nest. Then he waited there while the other went away for mud and stuck it on too.

"Whatever are they doing?" I said.

"I can't think," answered Nancy. "It's very funny!"

They kept on and by dinnertime the hole was much smaller.

"They're going to wall those sparrows in!" cried Dora, with a sudden startling inspiration.

"I believe they are!" exclaimed Nancy.

So we called Father and Mother and Miss Wilson to see, and they said they had never seen anything like it. It was quite evident that that was what the swallows meant, but the sparrows hadn't begun to suspect them yet.

We asked Miss Wilson and Mother if we might have a half-holiday to watch them. Miss Wilson was half inclined to say No, though it was clear she wanted to watch too—perhaps that was why—but Father and Mother both said it was such a wonderful thing that it would be a pity not to see it.

So we had the whole afternoon, after we had had our dinner, and that didn't take us long.

They kept right on, one watching and the other going for mud; and at last the sparrows began to see that there was something wrong.

The cock put his head out and would have come out altogether, but the swallow clung to the edge of the nest and beat him back with his wings. After this they tried to get out once or twice, but I think they were thoroughly frightened, for they didn't seem to try very hard.

By four o'clock the thing was done. The sparrows were quite walled up in the swallows' nest, and not the tiniest hole was left; and the swallows sat on the fence and twittered contentedly to each other.

"Well," said Nancy, "I never could have believed that birds could take a deliberate revenge like that."

"It serves the sparrows right," I said. "The little thieves!"

"But what will they do now? Will they leave them to starve to death?" asked Molly.

"They won't care," said Dora. "But it does seem rather hard."

"I think they're very cruel little birds," said Miss Wilson. "They're sitting on the fence and rejoicing in their work."

"Well, it was provoking to have those robber sparrows take their house, just as they'd built it so beautifully," said Nancy, "but it seems rather dreadful to starve them to death for it."

"They deserve to be thoroughly well frightened, anyhow," I said. "We might leave them in till Father comes home, let him see it, and then let them out."

"Yes. That would give them a lesson, I should think," said Nancy.

When Father came home, he was very tired, so we thought he had better have tea before we talked to him about the birds.

After tea we begged him to come out on the porch and see the nest.

"Don't you think we ought to let them out?" asked Dora. "It's a dreadful death to starve."

"How long has it been finished?" asked Father.

"Oh, about two hours," answered Nancy.

"Then I think you needn't fear starvation for those sparrows—they must have died long ago. The nest is so well sealed up they could not get any air to breathe."

"Oh, Father! Do you think so?" cried Molly, and she began to cry.

"Well, we'll see," said Father, and he made a hole in the nest with his knife, and put his hand in and took out first one sparrow, and then the other; but they were both quite dead.

Molly cried more than ever.

"Don't cry, child," said Father. "They must have died in a few minutes—and it was their own fault. They had no business there."

"I suppose the swallows will come back and have their nest now," I said.

But they never did. The nest stayed there empty all summer.

I wonder if it was haunted.

* * * * *

"The Swallows' Revenge," by Margaret Watson. Published in St. Nicholas, *July 1905. Original text owned by Joe Wheeler. Margaret Watson wrote for turn-of-the-twentieth-century magazines.*

THE SEA HORSE
OF GRAND TERRE

Charles Tenney Jackson

The great stallion seemed determined to kill Gaspar—yet look what happened during the hurricane!
And . . . what happened afterward.

* * * * *

Allesjandro, the seine-captain, first told the men at Chinese Platforms that the lightkeeper at Grand Terre Island was sick. One of the *Zelie*'s crew had gone ashore for water and reported that old Miller was "done beat out with feveh." The *Zelie* had two hundred dollars' worth of shrimp which a few hours' delay under the Louisiana sun would spoil, so the lugger sailed for the drying platforms, where Allesjandro told Mr. West, the camp boss.

And the camp boss turned with simple confidence to his sturdy sixteen-year-old son, who, that morning, was idling in the shade of the commissary with his chum, George Fernald.

"Better go see to the old man, Paul. The *Two Sisters* is flying the catch-flag, and the launch is going to tow her in. Landry will put you ashore, and you can hike up the beach with some lemons and stuff. See if he needs the doctor."

And blazing hot as low-lying Grand Terre appeared in the September calm, the boys were eager to go. Miller was a friend of Paul's. In half an hour, they had the few

delicacies and simple remedies which the camp possessed, and were on the launch speeding for the outlying reef. For a week, black, majestic storm clouds had swung about Barataria Bay, at intervals, for this was the time of the equinox, when the south coast had been swept time and again by the West Indian hurricanes. Still the shrimp luggers went out, and when the boys landed in the salt marsh, they saw the *Two Sisters*, limp-sailed and far on the gulf, but flying the red flag that told of a successful catch. The launch went on through Four Bayou Pass to meet her, while the boys turned up the six-mile beach to the lighthouse.

"Dad said that Gaspar, who takes care of the oyster beds here and keeps an eye on our cattle, might round up a couple of horses for us," commented Paul. "But all the stock seems to be miles away, and Gaspar isn't around his shack."

They passed the tiny, palm-thatched hut perched on a ten-foot platform above the tides. The mud beneath was trampled where the stock sought refuge from the sun, and here Paul pointed out a great hoof-mark.

"That's Big King's, the stallion that Father turned loose here when he went into this experiment with stock on the salt marsh. He has never been able to recapture him since. Gaspar complains that the white stallion hates him and chases him every time he goes ashore. The *Zelie's* crew say that they saw Big King follow Gaspar in his skiff away out in deep water, and that the Cajun [A contraction of the word *Acadian*, used in Louisiana to designate the descendants of the early French settlers exiled from Nova Scotia, as described in *Evangeline*.] was so scared that, finally, he dived over and swam to their boat. Gaspar sometimes declares he will shoot the horse or quit his job!"

"Must be a regular old sea-horse!" laughed George. "Is that him—that beautiful big white fellow over in the mangroves?"

"Yes," Paul whispered cautiously. "And don't provoke him to charge us—there isn't a place to escape him if he does!"

Two hundred yards way, the splendid creature stood, his eyes warily on the invaders. He snorted menacingly, his mane erect and tail spread, but he let them pass, and then charged magnificently down the wet sands to turn and watch them, with the surf breaking about his legs.

"What a grand old fellow he is!" cried Paul. "Father ought not to put him in charge of an oyster-digger like Gaspar—of course he'd hate him!"

It was dazzling noon when the weary boys reached the lighthouse. The oppressive calm made the heat in the marshy hollows intolerable, and they hailed with relief the sight of the keeper, whom they found lying on his airy platform. The keeper's eyes were feverish as he explained how, all morning long, he had watched them with his powerful glasses, which gave him the only diversion of his monotonous life. But he wasn't sick, he said—just a "touch o' sun," and he was chagrined to find that the *Zelie* had reported him ill. "Lighthouse folks ain't no business gettin' sick, ever," he declared.

All the same, he was glad to get the lemons and other things the boys brought, and when they tried to make him a cornstarch pudding, the ensuing hilarity seemed to hearten him wonderfully. When they came out on the gallery, he declared all this "cuttin' up had made him plumb well." But when the keeper gazed around, he fixed an intent look on the southeast.

"Your dad's goin' to have the launch at Four Bayou for you?" he asked. "Well, you boys better get off. The wind's scuddin' them clouds fast over there, and this is the hurricane month, remember. There's a sea running now, and—feel that? The air's twitching!"

And in fifteen minutes it was more than twitching. Out of the strange, calm oasis with the black clouds rolling up all about the horizon, there suddenly shot a squall from the southeast that tore the sand from under the boys' feet when they went down Mr. Miller's ladder. But they didn't mind the blow. They laughed and shook Miller's hand and promised to come the next day with the launch and make another pudding, and with raisins in it.

"Mebbe you will and mebbe you won't," shouted the old man. "It's time for a blow up from Cuby, and I reckon I'm better off here than you'll be on your dad's crazy platforms. You boys won't see old man Miller for a while, if a sou'east sea begins to pound over them marshes. In La Cheniere storm, there wasn't a thing above water except this light, from here to upper Lafourche. And your dad's platform villages—*pooh!* wasn't stick or stump left of any of 'em!"

The boys talked of the dreaded gulf hurricanes as they tramped on the harder sand, as near to the water as they could. On their left, the sand was already blowing from the dunes, and when they reached a little bayou which they had crossed dry-shod in the morning, they found the water pounding half a mile inland, and had to go around it. "The gulf is so shallow for miles out," explained Paul, "that the least little wind kicks up a quick seas."

But when they rounded the bayou and went over the low ridge, the wind was so fierce as to stagger them and whirl the loose sand around their feet.

"Whew!" cried George. "And just see how the water's rising, Paul! It's all through the grass there, and beyond—why, it's a lake!"

"Let's cut over on the bay side and see if the mangroves won't break the wind a bit," suggested Paul. "If it keeps on, we can't well walk against it." He reached a rise in the meadows and vainly stared at the pass which, two miles away, was hidden by the oncoming rain and scud. There was no boat in sight, and, northward, Barataria Bay was whipped to as furious a sea as was the outside water to the south. "It's there sure," Paul muttered, "but, if we *made* the launch, I don't think she'd live in that gale. But we can run to Grand Bank and put into that camp for the night."

He hastened on, not telling his friend all his fears. But from the highest dune they saw nothing except the oyster-guard's thatched hut, and, far off, near the mangrove clumps, a few of the cattle wandering with the storm.

"Ticklish business if we have to spend the night in this shack," George declared half an hour later, when, wet and tired, they reached the hut on the edge of the marsh and climbed the ladder to the door. Indeed, the sight was an evil one. The oyster-stakes had entirely disappeared, and the rising sea was pouring across the island in three places back on the way they had come. The pounding water against the piles made the shack reel, while every now and then portions of the thatched sides would be torn off, and go humming away in the gale. The boys went in and inspected the gaping roof; the sheets of rain reached every inch of the interior—they were as well off outside. Where Gaspar had gone they did not know; they concluded that he had abandoned his job—"Scared off by the big horse," said Paul.

"If the water keeps on rising, you'll lose all your stock," observed George. "But the launch—where do you suppose it is?"

Though night and darkness were coming on, they could see enough to know it held no boat. What had happened was that the launch, early in the afternoon, had broken its propeller in towing the *Two Sisters* and had then drifted until both boats grounded in the marsh, where the crew clung, half drowned, to the lugger's rigging through the night of the hurricane. The boys, huddled in what should have been the lee shelter of the thatch on the platform, noticed again how fast the shallow sea was rising. Grand Terre light was invisible in the storm, and it seemed that the whitecaps were speeding across the island everywhere except over the higher sand-ridge near them. Watching this, they saw the backs of the cattle moving through the mangroves, and then Mr. West's old bay mare. "The stock are coming back!" cried Paul. "The water's coming in from the pass now, and it's turned them." He looked apprehensively at his companion's face. "George, if it rises high enough to get a sweep at this shack over the bars, the platform won't last half the night."

"Your cattle are coming here, anyway. And look, the big horse is leading them!"

The stock had been accustomed to huddle in the shade of the platform hut, and now they were deserting the mangrove ridge to seek this bit of human companionship. The cows were mooing in a scared fashion as they waded, more than knee-deep, to the place. The two bay horses cast appealing looks up at the boys, and Paul called down encouragingly. Big King lunged about the piling and whinnied, watching off to the mainland. The frail structure trembled when the crowding cattle got under it.

"Better drive them out," George shouted above the wind. But this was impossible; and presently, as the darkness fell, the animals were quieter in the fierce rain, though the waves pounded over their backs, and the calves could hardly keep their footing.

Paul crawled back on the platform after an inspection of the base of the timbers. The sands were washing up badly, and the tramping hoofs assisted at the slow settling of the platform. Paul could touch the horses' necks from the floor, and once his fingers went lightly along the rough mane of the white stallion. The big brute turned about his fine, wary eyes at the boy. But he did not bite; he even seemed to crowd closer to his master's son. "Get over there—you!" Paul yelled. "Don't crowd against that post!"

He reached down and slapped the great horse and then dug him in the ribs ineffectually. King neither resented it nor obeyed. The boys lay full-length on the boards to avoid the wind, and in the last light saw their dumb companions half buried in the waves. Although the rain was not cold, they were shivering with exhaustion from the pounding wind and water. For an hour, the dark was intense. Then it seemed as if the rising moon broke the gloom a trifle, though the storm did not abate.

"It's still rising!" exclaimed Paul, after he had thrust a crab-net pole down by the piling. "And very fast, George. I wish it were daylight!"

Then, when he had crawled back to his wet comrade, there came a tremendous shock to the platform. They heard one of the calves bawl wildly and felt a rush and stagger of the animals beneath them. Paul jumped up and ran to the other end of the reeling platform, where an entire side of the thatched wall fell out into the sea.

"It's a big tree!" he shouted back, as George groped for his hand. "I was afraid of that, whenever the tide got high enough to bring the drift off the gulf side. Now we're in for it! It tore out three of the piles, and it's dragging at another. Come, let's try to get it off!"

Thirty-five miles away, the Southwest Pass of the Mississippi poured all the flotsam of the mighty river into the Gulf to be spread far along the sand dunes by the tides, and every southeaster sent this wreckage charging over the marshes. In every great blow the platform dwellers of Barataria dreaded this invasion. The boys vainly hunted for poles to fend off the tree pounding under their shelter. Some of the cattle had been knocked down and others were scattered; and Paul saw one of the mares go swimming off in the whitecaps to certain death. Above the wind they heard the frightened stock struggling for foothold in the sand and the groaning of the timbers. There was nothing to do. The shack, trembling, twisting, finally settled slowly back: the big cypress-tree had gone on, luckily. But presently a smaller one was battering at the piling, and more of the cattle were scattered.

"The other end of the platform is sinking!" George shouted. "Everything is gone there!"

They fought their way back just in time to see more than half the thatch hut tumble into the waves. Paul had saved a coil of half-inch rope from Gaspar's belongings, with the idea of tying fast some of the loose piles, but this was now useless.

"The rest of it will go for sure!" he muttered. "George, when it does, jump clear of the cattle and head southwest—" he looked helplessly off in the dark—"if we can swim to the mangroves, maybe we can hold on a little longer."

But to reach the ridge, even if it was above the breakers, was an impossibility, for one would have to swim directly into the storm. And the boys had lost all sense of direction. The next big shock from the driftwood sent them to their feet in a wild effort to leap free of the animals, although how many of them there still were they did not know. The last log crashed through the midst of them and left the platform tilted at such an angle that the boys could no longer walk on it. Paul slipped and went over the side to his waist, but he still clung to his rope. As he kicked to recover his footing, while George reached down to help him, he slowly became aware that his legs were over the wet, heaving back of Big King. His hold on the boards was slipping; the entire platform seemed to be coming after him.

But Paul was motioning wildly for his friend to slide after him. He was reaching around the big slipping boards to drag the rope about the big stallion's neck.

"If it goes," he shouted, "hang to the rope; maybe Big King will drag us free of the stuff."

He was working busily at the rope about the horse's neck when George was thrown into the water beside him. The stallion was plunging about with Paul firmly astride his back and George fighting to grasp the rope. Another instant and the wrecked platform slid down upon them, striking Paul in the side and dealing the horse a savage blow on the flank, driving him out from under the piles where he had fought to the last against the sea. He plunged on madly, with the water breaking over his back, to which Paul clung while he tried to drag his friend up behind him. They never would have succeeded if King had been on dry land. But the water and the small drift impeded his struggles to shake off the rope and the burden, and now he dashed into a depression where his hoofs failed to find bottom, and the waves swept entirely over him.

The panting boys clung to the rope and to each other. Paul was dragged off the back of the swimming horse, and then they both were thrown against him and regained a hold on his tough and heavy mane. But the whitecaps were almost drowning them. Big King reached a ridge and drew himself up where the water was hardly to his breast; then he plunged on in the teeth of the storm, swimming again. He knew where he was going well enough. While the foolish cattle drifted with the waves out to the open bay, the lion-hearted stallion fought his way seaward and to the mangrove ridge.

But before he gained it, the boys were all but washed off. Once, indeed, Paul felt his friend's hand slip from his. George went over the horse's flank and under the water, but he kept his grip on the rope. From his gasps, the rope was apparently all but strangling the stallion. When they reached another shallow, Paul leaned forward and loosened it. "Hold up, old fellow!" he muttered. "Hold up, and we'll make it yet!"

And the big wild horse actually twisted his shaggy neck knowingly under the boy's fingers as he eased the line! Paul got George on the animal's back again as they reached the mangrove ridge. The bushes, beaten by the hurricane, cut and pounded their faces, and the choppy seas broke through, churning the sands about them. But the water here was not more than three feet deep, and Big King fought through it.

Paul was anxious to stop him now. They were on the highest point, and no other refuge was possible. He began patting the horse and murmuring to him as one would to a pet colt, and, after a quarter of a mile of fruitless tramping, Big King suddenly rounded the thickest clump of mangrove and stopped, with his tail pointing into the gale.

"He knows!" whispered Paul weakly to his comrade. "It's the only shelter to be found. Now if he only lets us stay on his back!"

But apart from nervous and resentful starts and shakings, the horse did not stir. He seemed badly exhausted himself. The boys lay forward on his heaving back, Paul clinging to him, and George to Paul, and there the weary, dark hours passed. The sea was rising more slowly now. At times, King struggled deeper into the bushes as the sand washed from under his feet. And how the wind did blow! It was as if the air above them was full of salt water, and even with their backs to it, the boys could not speak without strangling. The lashing mangroves skinned their legs painfully, and the salt added to their suffering. But their chief fear was the rising water. They measured it time and again during the long night, but could never tell whether it was coming up or whether their live refuge was slowly sinking. The stallion changed his position whenever his legs went in too deep. "Old boy," muttered Paul, "you can manage this much better than we can."

Somehow, in his heart, he felt a hot and almost tearful love and admiration for the dreaded horse of the Grand Terre meadows. "If we ever get out," Paul told George, "I'll take him back to New Orleans and ride him. He's the biggest, bravest horse in all the world!"

"*If* we get out!" retorted George. "And I do believe the rain is quitting!" And with the ceasing of the rain, a slow lightening came over the waters. Yet not for hours longer, while the long, tugging swells surged through the mangroves and kept the tired boys ever struggling to retain their place, did it become light enough to be really day. And then they saw nothing in any direction but gray sky over the stormy sea. For two hundred yards, the higher mangroves were above the flood. Of the palm-thatched hut and the platform not a stick remained, nor was a single one of the cattle or either of the two mares in sight.

"Nobody but Big King," muttered Paul, "and you and me, George! I'm going to get down and pet the old fellow!"

He swung off in water to his armpits and went about to King's head. The horse bared his teeth, and then slowly, with lessening pride, allowed the boy's hand to stroke his muzzle. "Old man," whispered Paul, "you weathered the blow for us, didn't you!"

And the strangest thing was that, when the boys were tired of standing in the water, the great creature allowed them to climb again on his back. At last the wind died out, and when the first glint of sun broke through, it could be seen that the sea was not rising further. Big King began nibbling at the mangroves, while the exhausted boys half dozed and watched the waters to the north. It was two hours before they could see anything two miles distant, and knew that the "hurricane-tide," so feared by the shrimpers, had turned again seaward. Drift and wreckage were going out through the flooded pass. And, finally, almost at noon, Paul made out the little gas steamer that ran from camp to camp, headed down from the direction of the platforms.

"It's looking for us, George!" he cried. "But Dad—he'll never dream we lived through it all!"

They watched the boat with weak yells of jubilation. A mile away, Big King's white flanks caught the attention of the steamer men. Then they saw the boys, and, fifteen minutes later, Paul and George were united with Paul's father. "Dad, your old sea-horse did it!" cried the son. "I'm going to get him off this island, for he deserves better things. He ought to get a life-saving medal!"

"I'll wager," laughed Mr. West, "you'll never lay hands on him again."

And the boys never did, though they made three trips to Grand Terre after the sea went down, first to attend to old man Miller, and then to tame the great white horse. Big King did not molest them; he even let Paul come close enough to reach out a loving finger to his nervous muzzle. But that was all; at sight of a halter or the motion of a hand to his neck, he was off, again charging magnificently down the wet sands to turn and watch them, with the surf breaking about his legs. To the end of his days he remained the lonely and wild sea-horse of Grand Terre.

* * * * *

"The Sea Horse of Grand Terre," by Charles Tenney Jackson. Published in St. Nicholas, *May 1914. Original text owned by Joe Wheeler. Charles Tenney Jackson was a prominent early twentieth-century journalist, short story writer, and novelist.*

Eben Brown's Combination Snake

Author Unknown

* * * * *

Tom Wilson's hog was undeniably the top killer of rattlesnakes in all Pike County, and had the rattles of the deceased to validate the achievements. But along comes Eben Brown with a challenge that appeared not only stupid but insane to the proud owner of the hog. What followed seemed right out of the pages of Mark Twain stories—but isn't.

* * * * *

"Eben Brown never forgave Tom Wilson for deciding against him in the great Pike County handicap snake race," said Deacon Todgers, when the boys asked him for a tale of life in the old Pike County days.

" 'I'm a good man, and forgiving,' said Eben earnestly the day after the race, 'but I'll get even with Tom Wilson even if I develop premature baldness trying to think up some scheme. And when I strike, I will aim at his tenderest part.'

"Now if there was one thing Tom Wilson thought more of than anything else it was his pet hog. There's no denying he was an animal of parts, an animal that would have been a source of joy to his owner in any part of the world. The hog could count up to ten, he could spell out his name with blocks, and do other things which are not generally included in the repertoire of a fat, placid-looking, middle-aged hog. But the long suit of that hog, and the thing that most delighted the soul of Tom Wilson, was his ability to kill snakes.

" 'There isn't but one thing for a snake to do when my hog comes in sight,' Tom used to say, with a look of honest pride on his face. 'And that is to commit suicide. For if he lingers on the premises, he will only meet with a painful death and add to the laurels of that noble animal of mine and his worthy owner.'

"One evening, when there was quite a crowd in the tavern and Tom Wilson was holding forth on the beauty and numerous attainments of his gifted animal, Eben Brown came in. He listened in a sort of sneering way and finally broke in on Tom's eulogy.

" 'A hog's a hog,' said Eben, sort of contemptuously. 'Even when he has a talk-ative owner, who is able to goldbrick people into thinking he's an animal of talents.

And I don't deny that your humble pet can fumble about with blocks and delude strangers into believing he can spell. But when it comes to killing snakes, I don't think he's any great shakes.' "

"Well, Tom Wilson was one of the most grieved and shocked men in the county at hearing his pet run down in that manner. For Tom had educated and trained his hog until it was almost like a child to him.

" 'Don't go around blaspheming the good qualities of a dumb animal that knows more than anyone by the name of Eben Brown can possibly appreciate,' answered Tom in his most emphatic manner. 'Out in any storeroom are skins and rattles of hundreds of snakes that bear testimony of the sincerity and single-heartedness of my pet's good work as a reptile slayer. It's easy for the envious to throw conversational jibes at my hard-working, innocent-minded pet. But I haven't heard you make any remarks about wishing to back your heretical opinions with coin of the realm.'

" 'I don't want to bet against any alleged evidence you may bring forth as to your hog's record,' said Eben, still sort of sneering-like. 'It would be easier and quicker to get rid of my money by putting it in an envelope and shoving it under your door. But if you want to bring your prize animal out in the open, I might make a small wager with you. But I don't suppose you would care to match him against anything larger than a garter or milk snake, and he could probably beat one of them.'

"Tom was mad clear through.

" 'Milk or garter snake!' he exclaimed, angrily. 'It's at killing rattlers and black-snakes that my hog has won honors and records for himself and good money for his owner. I'll back him against any snake in Pike County and take up any bet you choose to make. It's robbing your family to do it, but it is the only way to keep the money in the county and prevent you from buying gold bricks with it.'

"So it was agreed to match the hog against any snake Eben might produce, the fight to take place in the big field at the side of Tom Wilson's tavern. I was considerably worried over what I considered Eben's foolishness.

" 'Tom is a vessel of wrath,' I told Eben, 'and it's a worthy and pious scheme to try and deplete his pocketbook. But I can't see but that your present game is going to result in the transfer of painful experience to Eben Brown and good money to Tom Wilson. For, despite your jeering words the other evening, there is no manner of doubt that hog is a wonder at killing snakes. I've seen him wade through a bunch of rattlers rag-time step. And it's just fun for him to add to the list of blacksnake fatalities.'

"But Eben Brown, instead of seeming worried, took me into the house and showed me an item in a paper about a man that lost a finger and by quick work the doctors had grafted in the finger of a healthy individual, who had more use for money than fingers.

" 'There,' said Eben, with the air of a man who had made a great discovery, 'there is the essential idea in my plan that will lead in the downfall of Tom Wilson's hog and will teach his owner not to make disparaging remarks about the good man who trained the original Pike County racing snake.'

"Even then I couldn't see what Eben was driving at.

" 'How grafting fingers on a prize hog will help you is a problem far beyond Deacon Todgers,' I replied, puzzled-like. 'Even if Tom will consent to let you interfere with the unalienable right of every hog to go through life ungrafted, a few fingers more or less won't retard the snake-killing energies of that hog. And do you propose to sacrifice your own toil-worn digits in the interest of science and Pike County snakes?'

"Eben was vexed at my keen sarcasm.

" 'The hog isn't my prize card, deacon,' he answered impatient-like. 'Snakes are what I'm putting my money on. I don't deny that Tom's pet is a recordmaker as a slaughterer of ordinary snakes. But when he runs up against your uncle Eben's grafted, double-snake combination, he'll think he's fighting the creation of some weird dream. And, even if he is a hog of talents, I don't believe his nerve will be strong enough for him to do efficient battle. Pet hogs will find themselves outclassed when they bump up against science and Eben Brown's intelligence. A grieving spirit for Tom Wilson and a decent burial for the prize hog are going to be the results of the coming contest.'

"At that I couldn't understand how Eben would make good with his grafting scheme.

" 'Endless chains are all right in their way,' I warned him, 'but I don't see how you are going to apply the principle to Pike County rattle and blacksnakes. And even if you do succeed in grafting together a few snakes, it's my belief it will interfere with their fighting qualities.'

" 'I don't propose to make a living rope of Pike County rattlesnakes and have it hang the hog, deacon,' Eben said, in a slow, earnest fashion, like a man explaining things to a child. 'It's by working on the snake's moral qualities and worrying him by the novelty of the game that I expect to win coin and honor and revenge. If you were wandering through the woods and met a blacksnake, you would probably kill it. If you ran up against a rattler, the sight wouldn't cause you extreme joy, but still you wouldn't be especially alarmed. But if you met a blacksnake with rattles, you would probably hunt a tree. And that is what will be the effect on the mind of Tom Wilson's hog when he prepares to do battle with my champion.'

"So Eben caught a big blacksnake and a rattler of corresponding size. Then he cut their tails off and grafted the rattling end of the rattlesnake on the blacksnake. The blacksnake didn't take kindly to the operation, but his wishes weren't consulted. Eben kept the combination snake in a long narrow box, where he couldn't do much twisting. In a week the grafting had taken effect, and Eben was the proud possessor of an animal that was unique in the history of Pike County—a big, bad-tempered blacksnake, but equipped with an exceptionally fine set of rattles.

"Eben was the proudest man in the county.

" 'Coming generations will bow their heads in reverence at the name of Eben

Brown, the able and modest old man, who first recognized the possibilities of animal grafting,' he said proudly. 'This attempt of mine is the opening wedge for a long line of discoveries. It won't be many years before we shall see dogs with cats' heads and tails, giraffes with eagles' wings, and all sorts of things that seemed impossible until your uncle Eben entered the scientific arena. Evolution has done big things for the progress of this world, but even evolution will have to take a backseat and blushingly retire when your uncle Eben's brain begins to get in its fine work.'

"Well, putting evolution on a backseat seemed considerable of an achievement for a little, bald-headed old man, but it can't be denied that his snake was the real article. It took the snake a few days to sort of get used to himself. Most of him was a blacksnake, but the rattles were there, and in good working order. When the snake got excited and made a sudden move, the rattles would give out a whirr. Then the snake, being at heart a blacksnake and a natural enemy of the rattler, would whirl around and look for a fight. But the only rattles in sight were his own. So the snake would calm down. But the effect of being so often stirred up was to make it about as bad-tempered a reptile as could be found in the state. He was a powerful big creature, always ready to fight anything that walked or flew. And anyone who ran across him was apt to think he had been indulging too freely in stimulants and give the ugly-tempered combination snake a good wide berth. Eben was the only one who could do anything with the snake, and Eben kept him in the box most of the time, for if anything went wrong, the snake would fly at him.

" 'Viewed as a fighter,' Eben said, sort of sorrowfully, 'that combination reptile of mine certainly is a wonder. But he isn't an animal that will ever take kindly to fond caresses or make heart-to-heart friendships.'

"When the day for the fight came, Eben toted his snake to the field of battle in a big box. Tom Wilson and his prize hog were on hand and ready for business. Tom was gloating over the money he expected to win from Eben, but even more at the manner in which he felt certain his hog would vindicate his reputation as a snake-killer. For it never occurred to Tom that his pet could be beaten.

" 'Whenever you are willing to deliver that poor snake over to death,' said Tom, in his sneering way, 'just shove back the lid of your box. My hog has a number of important business engagements, and he would like to dispose of your deluded victim as quickly as possible.'

"Eben didn't make any reply, but pushed back the cover of the box. Out shot his combination snake. The snake was always short-tempered, and just then he was pretty well stirred up at having been carried around in a hot, stuffy box. He didn't waste any time in formalities, but started for the hog. The hog, as soon as he had seen the snake, had begun to stroll towards him in the nonchalant manner of a hog who would kill a dozen snakes just as his early morning exercise. But when he got closer to the snake, the hog stopped in a puzzled way. The rattles were whirring that would seem to indicate a rattlesnake. But the head and body bore all the signs of a black-snake. You could see the prize hog's mind was disturbed. Besides this, he was accustomed to seeing snakes of every kind hunt cover when they saw him. But this new variety of reptile seemed to be ready and anxious for a fight. The hog prepared to step on the snake near the head, after his regular manner of killing rattlesnakes. Then he took another glance at the head and body and tried to change his plan of attack. The result was that he wasn't more than half prepared when the snake reached him and was a pretty well alarmed hog. At the last second the hog shot out his forefeet. His move would have been all right if he had been up against a slow-moving rattler. But it didn't count against a combination snake that was quicker and stronger even than the ordinary blacksnake. The snake made a spring, seized the prize hog by the throat and began choking him to death in the calm, business manner of an extra big combination snake. And when the snake finally let up on his grip, an honorable burial was the only thing needed for the prize pig.

"It was the first time Tom Wilson had ever been hit very hard at the betting game, and he was a disgruntled individual when he handed the money wagered over to Eben Brown. But besides feeling the loss of the money, he was honestly grieved at the thought of his pet's defeat and death.

" 'Rattlers were easy for my poor, deceased pet,' said Tom sorrowfully. 'Black-snakes had no terrors for him. But when he ran up against that combination article he was evidently out of his class. Defeat was his portion, but not disgrace. For he died on the field of battle.'

"But Eben Brown fairly bubbled over with jubilant joy.

" 'Prize hogs are all right in their day and generation,' exclaimed Eben triumphantly, 'but when they match themselves against science and your uncle Eben's massive mind, what chance have they? Evolution had to take a backseat. And if evolution, why not prize hogs?' "

* * * * *

"Eben Brown's Combination Snake," author unknown. Published in Nor'-West Farmer, *December 5, 1902. If anyone knows the name of the author, please send to Joe Wheeler (P.O. Box 1246, Conifer, CO 80433).*

The Canary's Siege

Mary D. Leonard

The canary had no intention of joint-tenancy. The wrens disagreed—mightily! Which would win?

* * * * *

"Danny," the canary, had always enjoyed the long summers on the front veranda, where his roomy cage was hung in early May. Having no mate, he comforted himself with an interest in all the other feathered folk who came about his home near enough to be seen and heard. He began to imitate their notes. He soon learned the song of the oriole whose nest hung in a maple tree close by, the whistle of the old green parrot across the street, and the twitter of the little chickens whose mothers sometimes led them into the front yard.

One morning in midsummer, there arrived among the honeysuckles a pair of house-wrens, bent upon finding a place for a new home. Danny watched the noisy visitors with interest, and attempted an imitation of their notes. The wrens, however, flew into a rage instantly, and, alighting on the cage, silenced the astonished canary with a stream of angry chatter such as he had never heard before. Moreover, their examination of the cage put a new notion into their heads: they decided that on its flat top they would build a nest, and live on the roof of a gilded palace, if not inside one. Away they flew, and in a jiffy they were back again, and had carefully

arranged a foundation of twigs on the top of the cage. Danny looking on in amazed silence. But the invasion of his premises was not to be permitted, of course, and as soon as the insolent little squatters flew off for more building material, Danny dragged through between the bars all the sticks they had arranged. Back they came presently with more twigs, and at once discovered what had been done in their absence. Instantly they dropped their sticks and in a great passion began an attack on the poor canary, who curled up, a trembling little ball of yellow fluff, on the floor of his cage, just out of reach of the long beaks they thrust with lightning-like swiftness through the bars. At last, having, as they thought, reduced the canary to a state of fear that would keep him from further resistance, they picked up their twigs, once more laid the foundation of their nest on the top of the cage, and went off for another load.

The canary, however, was not yet wholly subdued, and no sooner were the wrens out of sight than he again pulled their foundation sticks through the bars, and, when he saw his besiegers returning, prudently retreated to the only safe spot beyond the reach of their beaks. The rage of the wrens when they found their second foundation destroyed knew no bounds. Over the bars of the cage they ran, screaming and scolding, and trying to seize with their bills the almost paralyzed canary, or to drag through the bars such of their twigs as they could reach. Finally, they again rearranged their foundation, and Mistress Wren went alone for more material, while her mate remained to guard the foundation. The case of the canary was now hopeless; his strength was nearly gone, his courage wholly gone; and so his human friends, seeing the contest had reached this stage, came to his rescue.

The insolent invasion of the wrens was not to be borne, of course. Yet it seemed possible to make respectable and useful veranda-citizens out of these dashing freebooters, and plans were laid to that end. An old strawberry box was found, a top fastened over it, a hole was cut in one side for a door, and it was tacked inside the cornice of the veranda near the ceiling. Danny's cage was cleared of the wrens' building materials, the twigs being put into the box. When the wrens returned, the pair took in the new suggestion instantly. A long and noisy discussion followed; repeated investigations of the box, inside and out, were made, intermixed with much scolding of Danny and his rescuers. At last, however, the wrens decided to accept the concession offered, but, in order to assert their independence and their intention to manage the affair their own way, they scornfully scratched out of the box all the twigs that had been placed there as a hint, and proceeded with wholly fresh material to furnish the home. Their subsequent airs of having won a great victory were exceedingly diverting.

Danny's nerves were shaken, and his vanity certainly received a great setback; but in time he learned to listen to the wrens' boasting without fear, while they ceased to resent his perfect imitation of the softer notes of their song.

* * * * *

"The Canary's Siege," by Mary D. Leonard. Published in St. Nicholas, *May 1902. Original text owned by Joe Wheeler. Mary D. Leonard wrote for turn-of-the-twentieth-century magazines.*

THE MOUSE'S RANSOM

Author Unknown

This incredible true story dates back to the British occupation of Egypt and was chronicled in the pages of Frank Lesley's Popular Monthly *back in 1877. Its premise is almost staggering: that a tiny mouse, one of the smallest of God's creatures, should be capable of such thought and communication with man!*

* * * * *

Salih was an Arab boy, who frequented the harbor of Suez and earned a precarious living by renting that much-enduring beast, an Egyptian donkey, from his owner; having liberty, for the consideration of about four cents per diem, to exercise the devoted animal's legs and back to his [Salih's] heart's content, so long as those indispensable portions of the animal should not be seriously damaged. Though the first part of the contract was not always carried out with scrupulous exactitude, the latter certainly was; and on days when a Peninsular and Oriental Company's steamer, with a good cargo of passengers, was delayed an hour or two longer than usual, owing to obstructions in the canal, the donkey in question was persuaded, by screams, curses, and thwacks, to proceed from the quay to the hotel and back, with the rapidity of a flash of lightning, an almost incalculable number of times. As these, the principal objects of interest in Suez, are about four miles apart, it will be perceived that the unwilling industrious animal earned his provender (such as it was) tolerably well. In accordance with the usual custom of the genus donkey-boy, the ass was dignified with the name of a European celebrity and answered to the title of "General Booth." On lucky days, Salih managed to extract considerable sums from passengers fresh from England, whom he persuaded to take an airing on General Booth. The General was naturally vivacious and possessed of a good stride, a most valuable quality in the frequent donkey-races which passengers, tired of many days on a ship's deck, were wont to indulge in on landing. Besides, he was not particularly wicked, as is often the case with these much-provoked beasts; he was never known to drop suddenly, as though shot dead, just when at his highest speed, or to turn a somersault in the middle of a crowded street—accomplishments possessed by but too many of his brethren. "Oh, no," as Salih was wont to assure passengers in broken English, "General Booth always pious."

Now Salih lived in a little hut, in one of the back streets of Suez, in company with his mother and two or three small brothers and sisters. His father was dead, and the widow had little to live on but the earnings of her son. She herself was almost completely blind from that ophthalmia which is one of the plagues of Egypt, and could do little but plait rush-mats and small baskets. She had never been able to afford to send Salih to school; so that young gentleman remained in ignorance, not, however, blissful. He possessed the natural quickness of the Arab and secretly regretted his inability to read, write, and use those strange marks by which the clerks at the quay found out all about the numbers and quantities of articles. He had also a hankering to be *mauddab* (learned in poetry and rhetoric disputations) regarding which he often overheard in the marketplace of Suez, when loitering there in the cool of the evening after sunset, the time when Arabs sit out in the street and discuss life in general.

As time went on, his yearnings after knowledge increased, and he one day, when unusually flush of cash, bought an old *Koran,* at the mysterious characters of which he would gaze with admiration and astonishment for hours together, whenever the moon was bright enough. He was too poor to indulge in oil for reading purposes. If he could but afford a few lessons in reading! Alas! there was no one among his own class who knew more than himself, and how could he find the time and the money for school?

He would sometimes, when driving his donkey to and fro, loiter for a minute or two at the corner of the street where there was a school. Inside squatted the little scholars on the floor, each with his book, his reed pen, and his small bottle of thick ink. The master sat cross-legged at the front of the room, with (as it seemed to Salih) a mighty array of books around him. Texts from the *Koran* ornamented the walls, texts written in every variety of Arabic calligraphy, that most artistic effort of scribes. Salih's eyes lingered longingly on those wonderful and sacred curves, on which local religious art had expended all its powers. Could he but learn to write like that! And then to listen to the boys reading, each his appointed task, in such an easy, fluent manner, as though the book were inside him, not outside; a familiar part of himself, not something foreign and mysterious! And the noble sound, too, of the ancient and holy words, so different from *his* Arabic! Then he would stir up his donkey, and go on his way, sighing.

When the great steamers landed their many passengers, and these lounged about the streets or by the canal, many of them, he saw, carried books in their pockets and took them out to read for amusement when they had nothing else to do. A gentleman in spectacles was one day thrown from General Booth's back, owing to the snapping of the girths when the donkey was entering the hotel courtyard at full speed. Out of the pockets of the rider flew two books and a newspaper; and the books had green and red bindings and pretty paintings on their outside, while the newspaper was full of pictures of men and women, and towns and ships. Wonderful to think that such beautiful things were made among the English, only to amuse them! Yes, it must be the knowledge they possessed that made them rich and powerful, so powerful that he had heard it said that great Sultans were among their servants! Ah! knowledge was a fine thing! But how to get it? It lived in books locked up securely from all who had not the key, the art of reading with understanding.

Now, one evening, when the moon was high and bright, Salih sat in his mother's hut with the *Koran* in his hand, looking wistfully at the long lines of well-ordered letters grouped into larger or smaller bands of words in the great army of each page, just like the soldiers who sometimes exercised on the sands outside the town. His mother and the other children were asleep, and he was in sole possession of the little outer room. He had been meditating sadly on the apparent impossibility of obtaining an education and had fallen into a kind of doze, when his attention was aroused by the proceedings of two mice which were scampering across the floor, inspecting every square inch in search of some minute particle of edible matter, no easy thing to discover in that poverty-stricken abode. There was a kind of impudence about these mice, which he had never observed in others of their species and which fascinated him in spite of the mournful thoughts that held possession of his mind. They marched around him (for he remained motionless) and sniffed at the hem of his dirty garment, as though desirous of making his acquaintance. It happened that close by his side lay a small brass basin commonly used for some domestic purpose. Watching his opportunity, he overturned this basin so quickly and cleverly, that one of the mice was caught beneath it, imprisoned in the brazen trap. The other fled, but soon returned and commenced making vigorous assaults upon the strange dome which had descended so rapidly on its comrade. Finding this in vain, it retreated to its hole.

It came forth again after an absence of a few moments, holding something in its mouth; the something was heavy, for the mouse appeared to carry it with difficulty. It was round, too, and glittered slightly when the moonbeams fell upon it. Up to the side of the basin, not far from Salih, advanced the mouse with its burden, which it deposited on the floor and then retreated a short distance. Halting a yard or two off, it sat up and looked intently at the boy.

Salih reached out his hand and picked up the object which the mouse had brought. It was—yes—there could be no doubt, it was—a piece of gold, an ancient coin, a *dinar* of the old Sultans of Egypt, who had reigned before the Turks were heard of. Evidently, the mouse intended it as a ransom for its imprisoned friend.

There is a belief very prevalent among Orientals that any extraordinary boldness on the part of mice is a sure sign of their possessing a treasure of some sort. Capital is supposed to confer upon them the same independence of demeanor which it does upon human beings. These mice had displayed extraordinary impudence in their approach of him; therefore Salih was confident that there must be more money in their hoard than the single *dinar* which had been produced. He therefore replaced the coin where the mouse had laid it and shook his head, in order to convey to the expectant animal that more must be forthcoming before a release could be granted to the captive.

After waiting a little, the mouse retired with a disappointed air, but reappeared quickly with another *dinar,* similar to the first, in its mouth. This it deposited on the floor by the other and sat up in a suppliant attitude, as though asking for pity and consideration. The boy's cupidity and hope now began to rise together, and he had no thought of liberating his very profitable prisoner until perfectly sure that he had exacted the uttermost farthing which the pair could command. So he continued to maintain a stern and unyielding countenance, on which the petitioner could perceive no sign of compassion.

A third journey to the hole took place, and a third coin was produced. The same silent show was repeated, and the drama proceeded as before between the two actors. Sometimes the mouse would sit for a longer period than at others, in the hope, apparently, that the extortionate youth would either pity, or become wearied with long waiting. But finding these expectations dashed, it would again return to the treasure house for another *dinar.* Salih, when telling the story afterward, asserted that its expression saddened perceptibly with each journey it took. The floor was eventually strewn with gold pieces, the original glittering hue of which had been dimmed by long neglect, and the deposits of centuries of mold; here and there, though, brilliant flashes came from those parts of them that had been clawed by the mice when they turned over, and doubtless counted, their hoard.

When twenty-five separate journeys had been made to the treasury, and twenty-five *dinars* exhibited to the delighted gaze of Salih, the mouse departed and reappeared with—no coin, but an old leather bag or purse. Bringing this to a part of the floor where the moonbeams shone brightest, it carefully turned the receptacle inside out. There was nothing within. The bag was evidently the original source of the *dinars* strewed around, and it was also clear that no more were forthcoming. The poor mouse was bankrupt; and with a touching air of resignation, it seated itself by the empty purse and looked beseechingly at the master of the situation.

That young gentleman saw that the bottom of the poor creature's pocket, so to speak, had been reached. It had given its all for its companion's freedom. The sex of the animal was not distinguishable; it might be a bridegroom, imploring for the release of his captive bride; it might be a wife, begging for her husband's liberty. In any case, it had deserved well of Salih; and fully sensible of this fact, he raised the brazen basin and set free the palpitating little prisoner, which fled immediately, with the utmost precipitancy, rattling the coins in its flight to join its partner. Both lost no time in disappearing into the hole.

When all was quiet again, the boy sat as one entranced. Could the scene he had witnessed and taken part in be a reality? Was it not rather one of those deluding dreams which, he had heard, often came to torment the longing and mock the desirous? But there lay the gold on the floor. Yes, but perhaps he was still dreaming. He pinched himself once or twice to make sure that this was not the case. No, he was wide awake, there could be no doubt about that; so he got up and clutched the *dinars* with a feverish hand. He had never seen so many gold pieces together before; and, indeed, had seldom seen any at all. Many times did he pick up each one and turn it over, with its mysterious legend and royal cipher; and when he was at last convinced that he was *bona fide* master of twenty-five good, solid, heavy *dinars,* he could keep his own counsel no longer, and called to his mother.

The rest of that night and most of the succeeding day was spent in considering what should be done with this miraculously obtained windfall. At last it was settled that half of it should be spent in improving the external appearance and the internal comforts of their abode; and the other half should be devoted to the commencement of Salih's long longed-for education. Two days afterward he took his place among the lowest class of that school into which his admiring eyes had so often glanced.

Time has passed since then, and Salih is now a man. He is well-taught in all the wisdom that modern Egyptians possess, and may, perhaps, be a Pasha some day. And if you can find him in the bazaar of Suez, he will perhaps tell you in his own words this story of the "Mouse's Ransom."

* * * * *

"The Mouse's Ransom," author unknown. Published in Frank Leslie's Popular Monthly, *vol. 23, 1887. Original text owned by Joe Wheeler. If anyone knows the name of the author, please send to Joe Wheeler (P.O. Box 1246, Conifer, CO 80433).*

FINDING DUDE

Lon Bledsoe
as told to Rhonda Reese

Is this a horse story? A marriage story? A love story? A God story? Or might it be all of the above?

* * * * *

Had it not been for my cherished friend Marthanne Glenn, of Silver Spring, Maryland, this story would not be in this collection. She first sent it to me about twelve years ago; then when years passed and I didn't anthologize it, she'd send it again, reminding me that she cries every time she reads it. So . . . partly to get her to stop crying, here it is.

* * * * *

The first time Bart told me about his horse, Dude, I knew their bond had been something special. But I never suspected Dude would bring a wonderful gift to me.

Bart loved all animals, but Dude, the chestnut-colored quarter horse he received when he turned nine, was his favorite. Years later when his dad sold Dude, Bart grieved in secret.

Even before I met and married Bart, I knew about grieving in secret. My dad's job led our family to relocate every year. Deep inside, I wished we could stay in one place where I could have deep, lasting friendships. But I never said anything to my parents. Yet sometimes I wondered if even God could keep track of us.

One summer evening in 1987, as Bart and I glided on our front porch swing, he suddenly asked, "Did I ever tell you that Dude won the World Racking Horse Championship?"

"Rocking horse championship?"

"Racking," Bart corrected, smiling gently. "It's a kind of dancing horses do. Takes lots of training. You use four reins. It's pretty hard." Bart gazed at the pasture. "Dude was the greatest racking horse ever."

"Then why'd you let your dad sell him?" I probed.

"I didn't know he was even thinking about it," Bart explained. "When I was seventeen, I started a short construction job down in Florida. I guess Dad figured I wouldn't be riding anymore, so he sold Dude without even asking me. Running a horse farm means you buy and sell horses all the time.

"I've always wondered if that horse missed me as much as I've missed him. I've never had the heart to try to find him. I couldn't stand knowing if something bad . . ."

Bart's voice trailed off.

After that, few nights passed without Bart mentioning Dude. My heart ached for him, but there was nothing I could do. Then one afternoon while I walked through the pasture, a strange thought came to me. In my heart a quiet voice said, *"Lori, find Dude for Bart."*

How absurd! I thought. I knew nothing about horses, certainly not how to find and buy one. That was Bart's department.

The harder I tried to dismiss the thought, the stronger it grew. I dared not mention it to anyone except God. Each day I asked Him to guide me.

One morning, three weeks after that first "find Dude" notion, a new meter reader, Mr. Parker, stopped by while I was working in the garden. We struck up a friendly conversation. When he mentioned he'd once bought a horse from Bart's dad, I interrupted.

"You remember the horse's name?" I asked.

"Sure do." Mr. Parker said. "Dude. Paid $2,500 for him."

I wiped the dirt from my hands and jumped up, barely catching my breath.

"Do you know what happened to him?" I asked.

"Yep. I sold him for a good profit."

"Where's Dude now?" I asked. "I need to find him."

"That'd be impossible," Mr. Parker explained. "I sold that horse years ago. He might even be dead by now."

"But could you . . . would you be willing to try to help me find him?" After I

explained the situation, Mr. Parker stared at me for several seconds. Finally, he agreed to join the search for Dude, promising not to say anything to Bart.

Racking tracking

Each Friday for almost a year I phoned Mr. Parker to see if his sleuthing had turned up anything. Each week his answer was the same: "Sorry, nothing yet."

One Friday I called Mr. Parker with another idea. "Could you at least find one of Dude's babies for me?"

"Don't think so," he said, laughing. "Dude was a gelding."

"That's fine," I said. "I'll take a gelding baby."

"You really *do* need help." Mr. Parker explained that geldings are unable to sire. But now he seemed to double his efforts, and several weeks later he phoned.

"I found him!" he shouted. "I found Dude!"

"Where?" I wanted to jump through the phone.

"On a farm in Georgia," Mr. Parker said. "A family bought Dude for their teenage son. But they can't do anything with the horse. In fact, they think Dude's crazy. Maybe dangerous. But you could get him back real easy."

Mr. Parker was right. I called the family in Rising Fawn, Georgia, and made arrangements to buy Dude back for $300. I struggled to keep my secret until the weekend. On Friday I met Bart at the front door after work.

"Will you go for a ride with me?" I asked in my most persuasive voice. "I have a surprise for you."

"Honey," Bart protested, "I'm tired."

"Please, Bart. I've packed a picnic supper. It'll be worth the ride. I promise."

Bart got into the jeep. As I drove, My heart thumped so fast I thought it'd burst as I chatted about family matters

"Where are we going?" Bart asked after some time.

"Just a bit farther,"I said.

Bart sighed. "Honey, I love you. But I can't believe I let you drag me off."

I didn't defend myself. I'd waited too long to ruin things now. However, by the time I steered off the main highway and onto a gravel road, Bart was so aggravated that he wasn't speaking to me. When I turned from the gravel road to a dirt trail, Bart just glared.

Just whistle

"We're here," I said, stopping in front of the third fence post.

"Here where? Lori, have you lost your mind?"

"Stop yelling," I said. "Whistle."

"What?" Bart shouted.

"Whistle," I repeated. "Like you used to . . . for Dude . . . just whistle. You'll understand in a minute."

"Well . . . I . . . this is crazy," Bart sputtered as he got out of the jeep.

Bart whistled. Nothing happened.

"Oh, please, God," I whispered, "don't let this be a mistake."

"Do it again," I prodded.

Bart whistled once more, and suddenly we heard a sound in the distance. What was it? I could barely breathe.

Bart whistled again. Suddenly, over the horizon, a horse came at a gallop. Before I could speak, Bart leaped over the fence.

"Dude!" he yelled, running toward his beloved friend. I watched the blur of horse and husband meet like one of those slow-motion reunion scenes on TV. Bart hopped up on his pal, stroking his mane and patting his neck.

"That horse is crazy"

Immediately, a sandy-haired, tobacco-chewing teenage boy and his huffing parents crested the hill.

"Mister!" the boy yelled. "What are you doing? That horse is crazy. Can't nobody do nothin' with 'im."

"No," Bart boomed. "He's not crazy. He's Dude."

To the amazement of everyone, at Bart's soft command to the unbridled horse, Dude threw his head high and began racking. As the horse pranced through the pasture, no one spoke. When Dude finished dancing for joy, Bart slid off him.

"I want Dude home," he said.

"I know," I said with tears in my eyes. "All the arrangements have been made. We can come back and get him."

"Nope," Bart insisted. "He's coming home *tonight*."

I phoned my in-laws, and they arrived with a horse trailer. We paid for Dude and headed home.

Bart spent the night in the barn with his old friend. I knew he and Dude had a lot of catching up to do. As I looked out the bedroom window, the moon cast a warm glow over the farm. I smiled, knowing my husband and I now had a wonderful story to tell our future children and grandchildren.

"Thank You, Lord," I whispered. Then the truth hit me. I'd searched longer for Dude than I'd ever lived in one place. God used the process of finding my husband's beloved horse to renew my trust in the Friend who sticks closer than a brother.

"Thank You, Lord," I whispered again. "Thank You for never losing track of Dude—or me."

* * * * *

"Finding Dude," by Lon Bledsoe. Published in Women of Spirit, *November/December 1999. Reprinted by permission of Review and Herald® Publishing Association. If anyone knows the whereabouts of the author, please send to Joe Wheeler (P.O. Box 1246, Conifer, CO 80433).*

NEP

Walter K. James

Who but God can fathom the heart of a dog!

* * * * *

Nep was a big, shaggy Newfoundland dog. When he first became a member of my friend's household, he was an overgrown puppy, fond of fun, and, like all puppies, full of mischief. His great desire seemed to be to pull to pieces everything that came his way. Often, when observed, he would destroy the hats and umbrellas left by visitors in the hallway. He was, however, such a good-natured, loving fellow that it was difficult to be angry with him, and besides, he seemed so sorry after he had been naughty that one could not help forgiving him.

Nep became very much attached to the baby and always followed its carriage when the little one was taken out for an airing. When the child was nearly a year old, she sickened and died. Poor Nep was disconsolate for a long time.

Some time passed, and another little one, this time a baby boy, came to the home of my friends. At the first cry of the new baby, Nep went into ecstasies of delight. He took up his old position by the cradle and constituted himself little Harry's special guardian. As the child grew and was able to toddle around, Nep never left his side, and the mother learned to trust the little one implicitly in the care of the big dog. Whenever she went to seek the child, it was the dog's name that she called, and the

dog that answered. When little Harry was about three years old, it appeared that he and Nep wandered one day farther than usual, and in some way ended up on some railway tracks. The line ran on an embankment, the sides of which were overgrown with brambles. There was a curve in the railway a short distance away. Suddenly, beyond the curve, the sound of an approaching train was heard; but, unconscious of impending danger, the child stood motionless on the track. As the engine whirled round the curve, Nep suddenly realized the child's peril, and rushing at the frightened boy, rolled him completely off the track and down the embankment on the other side. The engineer had already seen the child, and the train slowed up as it approached the spot. The little one was lying below on the grass, his face and hands much scratched by the brambles; and Nep was standing over him, licking his hands and face. A neighbor who was driving by saw the situation, and picking up little Harry, took him home in his buggy. Nep trotted contentedly behind the carriage until his charge was safely home.

Sad to relate, when Harry was four years old, he caught the scarlet fever. The dog refused to leave the child's bedside, and when the little one died, Nep evinced signs of the deepest grief. He followed the casket to the grave. During the summer, little Harry's mother went every morning to the cemetery with a basket of fresh flowers to deck the dear one's grave. Nep always brought the basket, and waited to have the flowers placed in it; then, taking the handle in his mouth, he trudged to the grave with his mistress and waited patiently until she had arranged the flowers.

This was repeated every day for some months. One morning in the fall, the weather was inclement, and the lady was indisposed, so that she was obliged to relinquish the idea of going to the child's grave that morning. Nep could not understand what was the matter. When the hour came, he brought the basket to his mistress as usual. She said, "Nep, old fellow, I cannot go this morning, but you may go if you wish." Placing the flowers in the basket, she opened the door. Nep looked gravely into her face, and then, seeming to realize what was expected, he took up the basket and trotted of.

A little time afterward the sexton of the church was astonished to hear a dog barking at the gates, which were fastened. Coming out of his house, he saw Nep standing there with the basket in front of him. Knowing the dog well, the man opened the cemetery gate and let him in, then followed him at a distance to see what he would do. When the dog arrived at the child's grave, he put down the basket, and taking out the flowers carefully with his teeth, deposited them in an orderly manner on the little mound. When this was done, he took up the empty basket and solemnly trudged back home.

* * * * *

"Nep," by Walter K. James. Published in The Youth's Instructor, *March 10, 1898. Text printed by permission of Joe Wheeler (P.O. Box 1246, Conifer, CO 80433) and Review and Herald® Publishing Association, Hagerstown, MD 21740.*

Betty and the Bear

Priscilla Leonard

If Betty had been far away from towns and cities, in the wilds of Montana, Wyoming, or Alaska, she wouldn't have been surprised to see a live bear. But surely not outside her window in the city!

* * * * *

" 'Measure juice and add one pound of sugar to each pint. Boil from five to eight minutes. Put a few drops on a piece of ice, and if the jelly separates slightly from the water, it is boiled enough.'

"There—I've done all that," said Betty, "and if the ice test is sure, this jelly will certainly jell.

" 'Skim a second time, and put in tumblers'—that's easy enough. Oh, if this currant jelly turns out anything like as good as Aunt Sarah's, won't I be a proud girl when Mother comes home! It'll be the best surprise I ever gave her, to have the jelly-making off her hands for the season. I believe it's going to more than fill all the tumblers—dear me! What else can I use? Oh, well, these yellow bowls in the dresser will turn it out all right, and so will these old cups without any handles."

Betty rinsed them out, washed them in spite of their evident cleanliness, and poured the last of the jelly into them with her capable seventeen-year-old hands. Grandmother Forsyth had had just such hands, the family traditions ran, and had been able to do anything with them, from embroidering on India muslin to uphol-stering the parlor furniture. Betty had her grandmother's name, too, and the little locket and chain that Grandmother Forsyth had worn as a girl was around her neck, though hidden somewhat by the comprehensive cooking apron that covered her from head to foot. With her curly brown hair and her big hazel eyes, Betty looked, in that enveloping apron, like a little girl, not old enough to be attempting currant jelly. But that is where appearances were deceptive. Betty, all by herself, had been keeping house for two weeks, while her mother was away at Aunt Sarah's, and had made a brilliant success of it. "Harry and Esther haven't even had a cold," she re-flected, with pride, as she looked at her array of tumblers, lucent in the sun, "and Father says my rolls are as good as Mother's. I'd better not be too proud, though, or my jelly won't jell!" She stirred around the little kitchen, cleaning up, and getting things in order; for Harry and Esther would be home from school soon for lunch, with youthful appetites.

Suddenly, she heard a queer noise from the front porch—a tremendously heavy step, it seemed, and then a rattling of the screen door. She went out into the entry to see what it could be—and stood transfixed. In the heart of a city suburb and civiliza-tion, at noon, there stood a bear—a real, live bear, looking in at her, and prying cau-tiously at the wire door with nose and paw. It looked to Betty as the very largest bear she had ever seen, but she did not hesitate a moment. The screen door was bolted with a light bolt that might break. Betty ran forward, closed the inner door, and locked it. That would hold. But suppose the bear tried the windows? Could it really *be* a bear? Betty went tiptoe into the parlor and peeped out to see if it were not a hallucination. No—there was the bear, large, brown, shapeless, terrifying. He had concluded that he could not get in that way, and was now moving inquiringly to-ward the windows. Nothing but a little glass and wire were there to keep him out, for the outside shutters were fastened back, and Betty dared not reach out to fasten them.

The bear looked at Betty. Betty looked at the bear. In the animal's little red eyes there really seemed no active ill nature. Betty tried to remember all she had ever read about bears. Perhaps he was trying to get in, in order to get something to eat. Bears liked sweet things—here a great light burst on in Betty's mind, and she turned and ran to the kitchen, snatched up a bowl of still warm and liquid jelly, poured it into the long-handled dipper, rushed back into the parlor, lifted the window farthest from the bear a little, and pushed out the dipper. The bear snuffed, shuffled nearer, eyed the dipper curiously, tried the jelly with his nose like a dog, and began to lap it greedily, his little eyes closing with delight. Aunt Sarah's recipe suited his taste to a T.

A porch chair, with a stout wooden seat, was nearly underneath the window, at one side. Betty cautiously and slowly lowered the dipper so that it rested on the seat, and then left the bear to enjoy it, while she went back and emptied two more bowls into a long-handled saucepan. Opening the parlor window gingerly again, she poked this, too, under Bruin's nose, and left it on the chair, for him to gobble in at his ease. Then she rushed to the telephone and called up the police station. "Is the chief of police there?" she asked.

"He's out. Who's calling?"

"1608 Washington Street, Betty Forsyth. Please send a policeman right away. There's a large bear on our front porch, and—"

"What?"

"A large bear! A *bear*. B-e-a-r!" spelled Betty, desperately.

"Did you say a bear, miss? Why, it must be a dog—a big dog. It can't be a bear!" The policeman's voice sounded stolidly incredulous.

"But it *is* a bear, and he's eating all my currant jelly! Please, please send a policeman right away!" cried Betty.

"All right, miss."

The policeman at the station desk hung up the receiver and whistled softly to himself.

"The dog-catcher's what she wants. Just scared out of her head with one of them Great Danes, most likely. Hello!" as the telephone rang again. "Yes, this is the police station. No, the chief's out. *Bear*—looking for a bear? *Great Scott, has this town gone raving crazy?* Oh—yes—you're the zoo, are you? Well, your bear is sitting up this very minute at 1608 Washington Street, eating currant jelly. There's a young lady there scared considerable. Yes—I'm sending her two policemen. You'd better get the park guard to go over too. It's a big bear, isn't it? She said so. Oh, it's Buster, is it? Well, well, I wouldn't care to have Buster come up on my front porch when I wasn't expecting him. Yes—I'll hurry up the policemen, and tell them to take ropes and not to shoot unless they have to. So long."

Meanwhile Betty was hastily moving more currant jelly to the parlor. The bear was grunting amiably over his pans and licking them clean. While he was thus peacefully occupied with one, Betty gently put out another. Then she sped back to the telephone and called up the school. Harry and Esther must not come home to meet the bear. But alas! They had both started; and Betty went back to the parlor, to find that they, and a group of fascinated street boys, were now pressing against the fence, open-eyed, watching the proceedings on the porch.

"Don't come any nearer!" called Betty, from the window where the bear was not. "Run away, both of you. The bear might hurt you before you could get away!"

"Sho!" said one of the street boys. "We've fastened the gate. He can't get out 'less he climbs over. And he ain't goin' to move so long as you give him more jelly. I know him—he's ole Buster, out of the zoo, and he's an awful cross bear when he gets mad. Better keep feedin' him."

At this juncture the two policemen appeared on bicycles. "Hi! Look at the ropes! Goin' to lasso old Buster!" cried the boys, dancing in glee. By this time a crowd had collected as if by magic, and the two policemen, entering the gate, were cheered on by a dozen excited advisors.

"Go right in and tie him. He's eating so fast he'll never notice." "Throw the lasso from the next porch!" "Make a barricade of chairs so's he can't get away!"

But the policemen lingered outside the gate. Buster looked extremely large. His temper was known to be uncertain. Neither of them was an expert with the lasso, and neither of them cared to tie a rope around the bear's neck with his own hands. It is hard to say what would have been done had the park guard not arrived just at this moment. He took one look at the situation, opened the gate, walked in, and hurried past the porch round to the kitchen. The bear hardly noticed him, having just commenced his sixth bowl of jelly.

The guard knocked at the kitchen door, and Betty opened it in a trice. "Got anything that'll hold enough jelly to get Buster all the way back to the zoo?" said the young man. "Something that'll hold about a quart, with a handle?"

Betty took down a deep, long-handled double boiler from the hook above the sink.

"That'll do," said the guard. "Fill it full—my, it's a shame to waste good jelly on Buster, but the zoo'll pay for it." He started off round the house, halted by the side of the porch, holding the boiler out toward the still unsatisfied Buster, who turned, sniffed, and started toward the luscious lure. The park guard let him take one gulp, then made for the gate, and the bear followed instantly. The crowd scattered like chaff, and out into the middle of the road went man and bear, at ever-increasing speed. The policemen jumped on their bicycles and followed; the crowd ran behind. It was an exciting scene, and it kept up all the way to the zoo. Occasionally Buster pressed the guard too close, and then he was given a taste of jelly and another record dash made before he could get into his stride again. Finally, when the chase had enlivened three streets, the boulevard, and the park entrance, the guard slowed down permanently, and marched in with the boiler held behind him and Buster following like a dog, lapping out of it, and so absorbed that he was led in this fashion into his cage, and the door securely closed on him. Aunt Sarah's jelly had shown itself equal to its reputation before it even had time to jell.

As for Betty, she cleaned up the porch, got lunch for Harry and Esther, and counted up and covered her remaining jelly-tumblers with trembling fingers. There were only one dozen left—Buster had taken the rest. That evening a well-satisfied bear curled up snugly in his den; and a proud father held forth to the neighbors who crowded the porch, on how his daughter Betty, like her Grandmother Forsyth before her, was equal to anything, even escaped bears; while the jelly, jelled to perfection, became the witness, for the rest of the year, to this true story.

* * * * *

"Betty and the Bear," by Priscilla Leonard. Published in St. Nicholas, *June 1911. Original text owned by Joe Wheeler. Priscilla Leonard wrote for magazines during the first half of the twentieth century.*

A Barnyard Lesson

William J. Long

And they say—animals have no sense of humor!

* * * * *

The cattle were dozing peacefully together in the warm afternoon sunshine when Spotty, the yearling, came out of the bushes, where he had just butted a nail cask to pieces, to show them all his new horns. Behind them was the low mud-thatched stable; in front, a small yard, dotted with giant stumps and surrounded by a long fence, over which a bear had climbed the night before and carried off a pig into the spruce woods.

The excitement of the latter event had scarcely yet disappeared from the barnyard, floating away by slow degrees, like the mist that filled the little valley over the trout brook below the farm. All morning the cattle had been restless, keeping close together for safety, and wandering but a little way into the woodland pasture. Earlier than usual, they drifted back into the log enclosure, where they felt reasonably safe, and now lay, with the afternoon sun full upon them, chewing their cuds contentedly, tired after all the excitement, willing to rest and doze and forget all about it. It was just at this psychological moment that Spotty came in to show them his new horns.

Now the barnyard might have been interested in Spotty's horns were it not for two things: first, they were very little horns, rising only an inch or two above the tangle of Spotty's black poll; and second, they had already seen the horns once, and had them forced upon their unwilling attention a hundred times more by their proud owner. But to Spotty they were the wonder of the world. As they grew, he felt his strength swelling within him and took to butting things to show his superiority.

Since the wild clamor in the night, when the pig went squealing away in the grip of Bruin's arm, and all the cattle had bellowed their fear and defiance into the still heavens, Spotty had been full of the excitement. All day long he had kept close to Brindle, the big steer—who had once licked a bear in fair fight—only running off at intervals, when the cows or sheep came near, to plunge like a battering ram at an unoffending dwarf spruce, to show them all how he would have done had he seen the bear. And he followed Brindle homeward again till within easy reach of the yard, when he went off by himself to hurry up some lagging ewes and ever hungry cows, and to butt at every inoffensive thing in the pasture.

When they had forgotten all their night terrors in the sleepy sunshine and the peace of a full stomach, Spotty still kept up his demonstrations. First he attacked an old stump fiercely and filled the air with brown dust and flying splinters. Next he jumped at the nail cask, which he knocked into some bushes and pounded till scarcely a stave was left clinging to its hoops. Then he came back to the barnyard.

A dozen cows and twice as many sheep lay resting quietly. Spotty stole up to them and gave one after another a gentle dig in the ribs, as if to say: *See those horns, will you? If they had only had a chance at that bear, what would have been left of him?* If they were appreciative, he went on; if not, he turned his head and gave them a harder jab with his other horn, to show them that it was all true what he was saying.

Over in a corner Brindle, the big steer, was watching the proceedings with bovine calmness. He was too big to disturb. Over in the opposite corner Butts, a surly old ram that had more than once driven me out of his bailiwick and left the marks of his surliness strong upon me, lay chewing, chewing, chewing, like a beaver at an alder stick. He was smaller, not half as big as Spotty. Moreover, he was independent, afraid of nothing, and minded his own business. Spotty had more than once thought of reminding Butts of his new horns; but something in the cold yellow eyes of the old ram always made him sheer off before he lowered his head. This afternoon was the time to remind Butts that there were other horns in the world besides his own rough wrinkled ones. Spotty was full of his importance after his encounter with the nail cask. There was confidence in his step as he approached Butts, giving a dig and a mighty push at a stump as he drew near.

Sitting by a corner of the barn, out of sight, I watched the proceedings with growing interest. I knew the old ram better than Spotty did. To a casual observer Butts saw nothing; his glassy yellow eyes remained cold and expressionless as that of a dead codfish. But there was a change there, a cold gleam like the glitter of ice in February. As a boy, when I saw that look in Butts' eye, I used to grab a club or fill my pockets with stones and climb a stump.

Spotty came up behind him, lowered his head, and gave him a questioning punch in his thin ribs. There was nothing vicious or bossy in the movement, just a soothing, gentle reminder. *"Do you feel that, Butts? There's a horn for you. Wait till it grows a bit, and I'll make you ashamed of your own old spruce roots. If you had only waked me in time, I'd have taken care of your bear. What!"*—as the old ram apparently gave no heed—*"You don't think so? Then here's a better one."* And he swung his head and gave Butts a harder jab in his other poor ribs with the other wonderful horn.

Butts was getting up to his feet deliberately, still chewing, an awful glare in his cold yellow eyes. Slowly he backed off, chewing, chewing, to disarm suspicion, as if he only wanted to get away from such dangerous horns.

But his eyes were fastened on Spotty; he seemed to see right through him and concentrate his attention, like Bunsby, on the coast of Greenland. When he got his distance, he paused to measure it with his fishy eyes and survey the ground for roots and rough places. Then he stopped chewing. Suddenly he humped his back, his gnarled old horns went down, and he shot forward as if hurled by a catapult, covering the ground like a gray streak of shadow, opening and shutting like a big jackknife, or a terrier after a cat.

Spotty's head was half lowered, after his last reminder, when the gray streak reached him, rose on its hind legs, and hit him *bang* between the eyes. The shock knocked the poor innocent clear off his feet. He went over like a tenpin, first squarely backward, where he sat for an instant on his own tail, then all in a heap, as he collapsed like a wild duck struck in full flight.

Butts backed away again slowly, his eyes cold as moonshine. When he saw his opening between the kicking legs, he hurled himself forward again and hit the proud owner of the horns another awful *biff* in the ribs. It seemed to knock the poor calf to his feet again, for he dashed away with a half-frightened, half-winded bleat; and jumping up I caught one glimpse of his tail whisking out of sight in the low stable door.

Butts watched him till he disappeared. Then his eyes regained their usual glassy stare; he lay down just where he was before, to save the trouble of warming a new place, and resumed his interrupted digestion.

Too bad that animals have no sense of humor! The cattle rolled their cuds as if nothing unusual had ever happened, and not even a microscope could detect any flicker in Brindle's bovine stare as he watched the little comedy. But Spotty's new horns had lost all present interest in the barnyard.

* * * * *

"A Barnyard Lesson," by William J. Long. Published in Outing, *July 1902. William Joseph Long (1866–1952) was a Congregational clergyman, naturalist, and author of such books as* Ways of Wood Folk, Beasts of the Field, *and* Spirit of the Wild.

My Musical Mouse

Albert Bigelow Paine

A musical mouse? Surely you jest!

* * * * *

In one of my school readers—McGuffey's third or fourth, I think—there was the story of a musical mouse. As a child I read this tale with wondering interest. A little later in life I was to see it verified.

I was a boy of perhaps sixteen when I learned to play a few chords and melodies on the guitar. As I had mastered these for my own amusement and suspected that my pleasure was not always shared by other members of the family, I often retired to my own upstairs room to enjoy it alone. Here at length I found one listener, at least, who was attracted by my performance. Perhaps his ear for music was not very refined.

In one end of my room there was an old fireplace about which there lived a few mice—not many, for we had a band of cats that roamed over the house at will. One night, as I sat playing, I heard a slight noise on the hearth. Glancing down, I saw a very small and meager-looking mouse. It was crouched as if ready to spring. It faced me, and its eyes shone like small black buttons. As I stopped playing, it moved its head about uneasily, and seemed uncertain what to do. Presently it ran back into the wall, stopping every few inches as if to listen.

I watched where it had disappeared and began playing again. In a few moments I saw the glint of its eager eyes. Then it crept out, little by little, crouching in its former position on the hearth. I played on softly and sat very still. It crept closer and closer, and pretty soon sat upright, its forepaws crossed, and its head tipped a little to one side, in a pose that was both comic and pathetic. I struck a few louder chords, and it perked up instantly in an attitude of extreme attention. I mellowed the music and continued playing. Then it dropped down on all fours, and drew nearer until it reached my foot. Here it hesitated a moment, and looked up at me, or rather at the guitar, eagerly. I sat perfectly still, and made the best music I could produce.

Slowly, very slowly, it climbed up, clinging to my trousers leg. When it had reached my knee, it once more sat erect, staring straight ahead. It did not appear to see me at all. I stopped playing for a moment, and it seemed uneasy and half dazed, but did not offer to escape until I finally touched it with my hand. Then it ran away, though with evident reluctance.

As soon as I began playing it returned, and this time I allowed it to creep up my coat and out on my sleeve. Here it sat for a long time very still, only pricking its ears and tightening its muscles a little when I played briskly and louder. If I stopped and touched it, however, it would run just out of reach of my hand, and wait for the music to begin once more.

As the evening passed, my new acquaintance became so bold, or rather so indifferent to my presence, that I could stroke it; and it was only when I took it between my fingers and thumb that it struggled weakly for freedom. It seemed so small and puny that I concluded it must be sick or half starved. At bedtime I drove it gently back to its den near the fireplace.

The next evening I came prepared with food; but when it crept out again, as it did almost as soon as I began playing, it only nibbled a little at the cheese, and dropped it a moment later to listen. I decided that it was the musical genius of some family of mice, and that food to it was of less importance than the enjoyment of tune and harmony. So far as I know, no other member of its family ever interested itself in my playing. Perhaps the others even deserted the fireplace and left my little friend alone.

As time passed I grew very fond of this tiny mouse. Sometimes during the day I pushed bits of bread and cheese into its den, and in time it became very tame, and would come out and act in so many cunning ways that I passed many delightful hours in its society. Once I placed it under a glass tumbler, with a tack between the edge to give it air. It did not enjoy its captivity, and at last succeeded in overturning its prison. Sometimes it would scratch itself with its hind foot or with its tiny teeth in a manner that was as interesting as it was amusing. The moment I began playing, however, all antics ceased, and it would creep up as close to the guitar as possible.

I fear the fact of its becoming so adventurous brought it at last to a tragic end. One evening when I began playing, it failed to appear. I played over the things it had seemed to like best, softly, at first, and then louder, thinking that it might be in some remote part of the wall and out of hearing. Still it did not come, though I played over and over all the pieces I knew, sometimes kneeling down and striking the strings close to the entrance of its little house, while I waited eagerly for its appearance. Finally I went to bed discouraged.

Early the next morning I played again in front of its dwelling, but it did not appear. At breakfast I mentioned the matter to my mother. She was silent for a few moments; then she said, "If your room door was open yesterday, I am afraid you will not see your little friend anymore. I saw Pug coming downstairs during the afternoon."

Pug was our largest gray cat. He was at that moment sleeping contentedly before the fire. I choked down my breakfast as best I could. Then I went to my room and played softly, and cried; for, after all, I was only a boy of sixteen.

* * * * *

"My Musical Mouse," by Albert Bigelow Paine. Published in St. Nicholas, *August 1897. Original text owned by Joe Wheeler. Albert Bigelow Paine (1861–1937), author, editor, and literary executor of Mark Twain, was one of the most prolific and best-known authors of his time.*

THE DEBUT OF "DAN'L WEBSTER"

Isabel Gordon Curtis

Everything was going so well—until Dan'l Webster and his out-of-control gang of turkeys demolished Finch & Richards's big market.
Mr. Richards had—more than had—enough.

* * * * *

"I guess you can get the ell roof shingled now, 'most any old time," cried Homer Tidd. He bounced in at the kitchen door. A blast of icy wind followed him.

"Gracious! Shet the door, Homer, an' then tell me your news." His mother shivered and pulled a little brown shawl tighter about her shoulders.

The boy planted himself behind the stove and laid his mittened hands comfortably around the pipe. "Oh, I've made a great deal, Mother." Homer's freckled face glowed with satisfaction

"What?" asked Mrs. Tidd.

"Did you see the man that jest druv out o' the yard?"

"No, I didn't, Homer."

"Well, 'twas Mr. Richards—the Mr. Richards o' Finch & Richards, the big market folks over in the city."

"Has he bought your Thanksgivin' turkeys?"

"He hain't bought 'em for Thanksgivin'."

"Well, what are you so set up about, boy?"

"He's rented the hull flock. He's to pay me three dollars a day for them; then he's goin' to buy them all for Christmas."

"Land sakes! Three dollars a day!" Mrs. Tidd dropped one side of a pan of apples she was carrying, and some of them went rolling about the kitchen floor.

Homer nodded.

"For how long?" she asked eagerly.

"For a week." Homer's freckles disappeared in the crimson glow of enthusiasm that overspread his face.

"Eighteen dollars for nothin' but exhibitin' a bunch o' turkeys! Seems to me some folks must have money to throw away." Mrs. Tidd stared perplexedly over the top of her glasses.

"I'll tell you all about it, Mother." Homer took a chair and planted his feet on the edge of the oven. "Mr. Richards is goin' to have a great Thanksgivin' food show, an' he wants a flock o' live turkeys. He's been drivin' round the country lookin' for some. The postmaster sent him here. He told him about Dan'l Webster's tricks."

"They don't make Dan'l any better eatin'," objected the mother.

"Maybe not. But don't you see? Well!" Homer's laugh was an embarrassed one. "I'm goin' to put Dan'l an' Gettysburg through their tricks right in the store window."

"You be n't?" and the mother looked in rapt admiration at her clever son.

"I be!" answered Homer, triumphantly.

"I don't know, boy, jest what I think o' it," said his mother, slowly. " 'Tain't exactly a—a gentlemanly sort o' thing to do; be it?"

"I reckon I be n't a gentleman, Mother," replied Homer, with his jolly laugh.

"Tell me all about it."

"Well, I was feedin' the turkeys when Mr. Richards druv in. He said he heered I had some trick turkeys an' he'd like to see 'em. Lucky enough, I hadn't fed 'em; they was awful hungry, an' I tell you they never did their tricks better."

"What did Mr. Richards say?"

"He thought it was the most amazin' thing he'd ever seen in his life. He said he wouldn't have believed turkeys had enough gumption in them to learn a trick o' any kind."

"Did you tell him how you'd fussed with them ever since they was little chicks?"

"I did. He wuz real interested, an' he offered me three dollars to give a show three times a day. He's got a window half as big as this kitchen. He'll have it wired in, an' the turkeys'll stay there at his expense. Along before Christmas, he'll give me twenty-two cents a pound for 'em."

"Well, I vow, Homer, it's pretty good pay."

"Mr. Richards give me a commutation on the railroad. He's to send after the turkeys an' bring 'em back, so I won't have any expense."

Homer rose and sauntered about the kitchen, picking up the apples that had rolled in all directions over the floor.

* * * * *

A week before Thanksgiving, the corner in front of Finch & Richards's great market looked as it was wont to look on circus day: only the eyes of the crowds were not turned expectantly up Main Street; they were riveted on a window in the big store. Passersby tramped out into the snowy street when they reached the mob at the corner. The front of the store was decorated with a fringe of plump turkeys. One window held a glowing mountain of fruit and vegetables arranged by someone with a keen eye to color—monstrous pumpkins, splendid purple cabbages, rosy apples and russet pears, green and purple grapes, snowy stalks of celery, and corn ears yellow as sunshine. Crimson beets neighbored with snowy parsnips, scarlet carrots, and silk-wrapped onions. Eggplants gleaming like deep-hued amethysts circled about magnificent cauliflowers, while red and yellow bananas made gay mosaic walks through the fruit mountain. Wherever a crack or a cranny had been left was a mound of ruby cranberries, fine raisin bunches, or brown nuts.

It was a remarkable display of American products; yet, after the first *Ahh* of admiration, people passed on to the farther window, where six plump turkeys, supremely innocent of a feast-day fate, flapped their wings or gobbled impertinently when a small boy laid his nose flat against the window. Three times a day the crowd grew twenty deep. It laughed and shouted and elbowed one another good-naturedly, for the Thanksgiving spirit was abroad. Men tossed children up on their stalwart shoulders, then small hands clapped ecstatically, and small legs kicked with wild enthusiasm.

The hero of the hour was a freckled, red-haired boy, who came leaping through a wire door with an old broom over his shoulders. Every turkey waited for him eagerly, hungrily! They knew that each old familiar trick—learned away back in chickhood—would earn a good feed. When the freckled boy began to whistle, or when his voice rang out in a shrill order, it was the signal for Dan'l Webster, for Gettysburg, for Amanda Ann, Mehitable, Nancy, or Farragut to step to the center of the stage and do some irresistibly funny turn with a turkey's bland solemnity. None of the birds had attacks of stage fright; their acting was as self-possessed as if they were in the old farmyard with no audience present but Mrs. Tidd to lean smiling over the fence with a word of praise and the coveted handful of golden corn.

With every performance the crowd grew more dense, the applause more uproarious, and the Thanksgiving trade at Finch & Richards's bigger than it had been in years. Each night Homer took the last train home, tired but happy, for three crisp greenbacks were added to the roll in his small, shabby wallet.

* * * * *

Two days before Thanksgiving, Homer, in his blue overalls and faded sweater, was busy at work. The gray of the dawn was just creeping into the east while the boy went hurrying through his chores. There was still a man's work to be done before he took the ten-o'clock train to town; besides, he had promised to help his mother

about the house. His grandfather, an uncle, an aunt, and three small cousins were coming to eat their Thanksgiving feast at the old farmhouse. Homer whistled gaily while he bedded the creatures with fresh straw. The whistle trailed into an indistinct trill; the boy felt a pang of loneliness as he glanced into the turkey pen. There was nobody there but old Mother Salvia. Homer tossed her a handful of corn. "Poor old lady, I s'pose you're lonesome, ain't you, now? Never mind; when spring comes you'll be scratchin' around with a hull raft of nice little chickies at your heels. We'll teach them a fine trick or two, won't we, old Salvia?"

Salvia clucked over the corn appreciatively.

"Homer, Homer, come here, quick!"

Down the frozen path through the yard came Mrs. Tidd, with the little brown shawl wrapped tightly about her head. She fluttered a yellow envelope in her hand.

"Homer, boy, it's a telegraph come. I can't read it; I've mislaid my glasses."

Homer was by her side in a minute, tearing open the flimsy envelope.

"It's from Finch & Richards, mother," he cried excitedly. "They say, 'Take the first train to town without fail.'"

"What do you s'pose they want you for?" asked Mrs. Tidd, with an anxious face.

"P'r'aps the store's burned down," gasped Homer. He brushed one rough hand across his eyes. "Poor Dan'l Webster an' Gettysburg! I didn't know anybody could set so much store by turkeys."

"Maybe 'tain't nothin' bad, Homer." Mrs. Tidd laid her hand upon his shoulder. "Maybe they want you to give an extra early show or somethin'," she suggested cheerfully.

"Maybe," echoed Homer. "But, Mother, I've got to hurry to catch that seven-thirty train."

"Let me go with you, Homer."

"You don't need to," cried the boy. "It probably ain't nothin' serious."

"I'm goin'," said Mrs. Tidd, decisively; "you don't s'pose I could stay here doin' nothin' but waitin' an' wond'rin'?"

Mrs. Tidd and Homer caught a car at the city depot. Five minutes later they stood in front of Finch & Richards's big market.

"Mother," whispered the boy, as he stepped off the car, "Mother, my turkeys! They're not there! Something's happened. See the crowd."

They pushed their way through a mob that was peering in at the windows and through the windows of locked doors. The row of plump turkeys was not hung this morning under the big sign; the magnificent window display of fruit and vegetables had been ruthlessly demolished.

"What do you s'pose can have happened?" whispered Mrs. Tidd, while they waited for a clerk to come hurrying down the store and unlock the door.

Homer shook his head.

Mr. Richards himself came to meet them.

"Well, young man," he cried, "I've had enough of your pesky bird show. There's a hundred dollars' worth of provisions gone, to say nothing of the trade we are turning away. Two days before Thanksgiving, of all times in the year!"

"Good land!" whispered Mrs. Tidd. Her eyes were wandering about the store. It was scattered from one end to the other with wasted food. Sticky rivers trickled here and there across the floor. A small army of clerks was hard at work sweeping and mopping.

"Where's my turkeys?" asked Homer.

"Your turkeys, confound them!" snarled Mr. Richards. "They're safe and sound in their crate in my back store, all but that blasted old gobbler you call Dan'l Webster. He's doing his stunts on a top shelf. We found him there, tearing cereal packages into shreds. For mercy's sake, go and see if you can't get him down. He has almost pecked the eyes out of every clerk who has tried to lay a finger on him. I'd like to wring his ugly neck!"

Mr. Richards's face grew red as the comb of Dan'l Webster himself.

Homer and his mother dashed across the store. High above their heads strutted Dan'l Webster with a slow, stately tread. Occasionally he peered down at the ruin and confusion below, commenting upon it with a lordly, satisfied gobble.

"Dan'l Webster," called Homer, coaxingly, "good old Dan'l, come an' see me."

The boy slid cautiously along to where a stepladder stood.

"Dan'l," he called persuasively, "wouldn't you like to come home, Dan'l?"

Dan'l perked down with pleased recognition in his eyes. Homer crept up the ladder. He was preparing to lay a hand on one of Dan'l's black legs when the turkey hopped away with a triumphant gobble and went racing gleefully along the wide shelf. A row of bottles filled with salad-dressing stood in Dan'l's path. He cleared them out of the way with one energetic kick. They tumbled to a lower shelf; their yellow contents crept in a sluggish stream toward the mouth of a tea box.

"I'll have that bird shot!" thundered Mr. Richards. "That's all there is about it."

"Wait a minute, sir," pleaded Mrs. Tidd. "Homer'll get him."

Dan'l Webster would neither be coaxed nor commanded. He wandered up and down the shelf, gobbling vociferously into the faces of the excited mob.

"Henry, go and get a pistol," cried Mr. Richards, turning to one of his clerks.

"Homer"—Mrs. Tidd clutched the boy's arm—"why don't you make b'lieve you're shootin' Dan'l? Maybe he'll lie down, so you can get him."

Homer called for a broom. He tossed it, gun fashion, across his shoulder, and crept along slowly, sliding a ladder before him to the spot where the turkey stood watching with intent eyes. He put one foot upon the lowest step; then he burst out in a spirited whistle. It was "Marching Through Georgia." The bird stared at him fixedly.

"Bang!" cried Homer, and he pointed the broom straight at the recreant turkey.

Dan'l Webster dropped stiff. A second later Homer had a firm grasp of the scaly legs. Dan'l returned instantly to life, but the rebellious head was tucked under his master's jacket. Dan'l Webster thought he was being strangled to death.

"There!" cried Homer, triumphantly. He closed the lid of the poultry crate and wiped the perspiration from his forehead. "There! I guess you won't get out again."

"Who'd have thought turkeys could have ripped up strong wire like that?" cried the enraged market man, pointing to the shattered door.

"I guess Dan'l began the mischief," said Homer, soberly; "he's awful strong."

"I'm sorry I ever laid eyes on Dan'l," exclaimed Mr. Richards. "I'll hate to see Finch. He'll be in on the four-twenty train. He's conservative; he never had any use for the turkey show."

"When did you find out that they—what had happened?" asked Homer, timidly.

"At five o'clock. Two of the men got here early. They telephoned me. I never saw such destruction in my life. Your turkeys had sampled most everything in the store, from split peas to molasses. What they didn't eat they knocked over or tore open. I guess they won't need feeding for a week. They're chuckful of oatmeal, beans, crackers, peanuts, pickles, toothpicks, prunes, soap, red herrings, cabbage—about everything their crops can hold."

"I'm awful sorry," faltered Homer.

"So am I," said Mr. Richards, resolutely. "Now, the best thing you can do is to take your flock and clear out. I've had enough of performing turkeys."

Homer and his mother waited at the depot for the eleven o'clock train. Beside them stood a crate filled with turkeys that wore a well-fed, satisfied expression. Somebody tapped Homer on the shoulder.

"You're the boy who does the stunts with turkeys, aren't you?" asked a well-dressed man with a silk hat and a flower in his buttonhole.

"Yes," answered the boy, wonderingly.

"I've been hunting for you. That was a great rumpus you made at Finch & Richards's. The whole town's talking about it."

"Yes," answered Homer again, and he blushed scarlet.

"Taking your turkeys home?"

Homer nodded.

"I've come to see if we can keep them in town a few days longer."

The boy shook his head vigorously. "I don't want anymore turkey shows."

"Not if the price is big enough to make it worth your while?"

"No!" said Homer, sturdily.

"Let us go into the station and talk it over."

* * * * *

On Thanksgiving afternoon the Colonial Theater, the best vaudeville house in the city, held a throng that had dined well and was happy enough to appreciate any sort of fun. The children—hundreds of them—shrieked with delight over every act. The women laughed, the men applauded with great hearty handclaps. A little buzz of excitement went round the house when, at the end of the fourth act, two boys, instead of setting up the regulation big red number, displayed a brand-new card. It read, "Extra Number—Homer Tidd and his performing turkeys." A shout of delighted anticipation went up from the audience. Every paper in town had made a spectacular story of the ruin at Finch & Richards's. Nothing could have been so splendid a surprise. Everybody broke into applause—everybody except one little woman who sat in the front row of the orchestra. Her face was pale, her hands clasped and unclasped each other tremulously. "Homer, boy," she whispered to herself.

The curtain rolled up. The stage was set for a realistic farmyard scene. The floor was scattered with straw, an old pump leaned over in one corner, hay tumbled untidily from a barn loft, a coop with a hen and chickens stood by the fence. From her stall stared a white-faced cow; her eyes blinked at the glare of the footlights. The orchestra struck up a merry tune; the cow uttered an astonished *moo;* then in walked a sturdy lad with fine broad shoulders, red hair, and freckles. His boots clumped, his blue overalls were faded, his sweater had once been red. At his heels stepped six splendid turkeys, straight in line, every one with its eyes on the master. Homer never knew how he did it. Two minutes earlier he had said to the manager, desperately: "I'll cut an' run right off as soon as I set eyes on folks." Perhaps he drew courage from the anxious gaze in his mother's eyes. Hers was the only face he saw in the great audience. Perhaps it was the magnificent aplomb of the turkeys that inspired him. They stepped serenely, as if walking out on a gorgeously lighted stage was an everyday event in their lives. Anyhow, Homer threw up his head and led the turkey march round and round past the footlights, till the shout of applause dwindled into silence. The boy threw back his head and snapped his fingers. The turkeys retreated to form in line at the back of the stage.

"Gettysburg," cried Homer, pointing to a stately plump hen. Gettysburg stepped to the center of the stage. "How many kernels of corn have I thrown you, Getty?" he asked.

The turkey turned to count them, with her head cocked reflectively on one side, then she scratched her foot on the floor.

"One, two, three, four, five!"

"Right! Now you may eat them, Getty."

Gettysburg wore her new-won laurels with an excellent grace. She jumped through a row of hoops; slid gracefully about the stage on a pair of miniature roller skates; she stepped from stool to chair, from chair to table, in perfect time with Homer's whistle and a low strain of melody from the orchestra. She danced a stately jig on the table, then, with a satisfied cluck, descended on the other side to the floor. Amanda Ann, Mehitable, Nancy, and Farragut achieved their triumphs in a slow dance made up of dignified hops and mazy turns. They stood in a decorous line awaiting the return of their master, for Homer had dashed suddenly from the stage. He reappeared, holding his head up proudly. Now he wore the blue uniform and jaunty cap of a soldier boy; a gun leaned on his shoulder.

The orchestra put all its vigor, patriotism, and wind into "Marching Through Georgia." Straight to Homer's side, when they heard his whistle, wheeled the turkey regiment, ready to keep step, to fall in line, to march and counter-march. Only one feathered soldier fell. It was Dan'l Webster. At a bang from Homer's rifle he dropped stiff and stark. From children here and there in the audience came a cry of horror. They turned to ask in frightened whispers if the turkey was "truly shooted." As if to answer the question, Dan'l leaped to his feet. Homer pulled a Stars and Stripes from his pocket and waved it enthusiastically; then the orchestra dashed into "Yankee Doodle." It awoke some patriotic spirit in the soul of Dan'l Webster. He left his master, and, puffing himself to his stateliest proportions, stalked to the footlights to utter one glorious, soul-stirring gobble. The curtain fell, but the applause went on and on and on! At last, out again across the stage came Homer, waving "Old Glory." Dan'l Webster, Gettysburg, Amanda Ann, Nancy, Mehitable, and Farragut followed in a triumphal march. Homer's eyes were bent past the footlights, searching for the face of one little woman. This time the face was one radiant flush, and her hands were adding their share to the deafening applause.

"Homer, boy," she said fondly. This time she spoke aloud, but nobody heard it. An encore for the "Extra Turn" was so vociferous, it almost shook the plaster from the ceiling.

* * * * *

"The Debut of 'Dan'l Webster,' " by Isabel Gordon Curtis. Published in St. Nicholas, *November 1904. Original text owned by Joe Wheeler. Isabel Gordon Curtis wrote for magazines early in the twentieth century.*

LITTLE MAN FRIDAY

Clara Morris

Mother, at best, tolerated the mischievous dog with Robinson Crusoe associations—but all that changed one never-to-be-forgotten day!

* * * * *

A babyish voice outside called, "Fwiday! Fwiday! Oh-h-h, Fwiday!"

Then there was a piercing whistle, followed by a boy's voice at highest possible pitch crying: "Friday! Friday! Friday!"

Mrs. Ames twitched her shoulders impatiently. She was distinctly cross, for she was in the midst of the misery of making jelly that wouldn't "jell," and as the calls of her two children came to her ears, she exclaimed: "For mercy's sake, just look at that glass of jelly, nearly cold and no thicker than cream! And all my life I've despised the woman that had to stiffen up her jelly with gelatin! Well, serves me right for beginning a thing on Friday! Nothing good ever came to anyone on Friday!"

I laughed and said, "Didn't Harry's dog, Little Man Friday, come to you on that day?"

"Yes," she snapped, "he did, if you call *him* anything good; and he came in a storm that tore off the shingles and let in the rain and spoiled the ceiling of my spare bedroom! No, nothing good ever comes to anyone on Friday, and—"

Just then there rose upon the air a cry of doggish anguish, and I ran out to see what was the matter with Little Friday Ames, whose high and sharp *ki-yi ki-yi!* expressed great terror or pain.

The front yard was separated from the back by a high, close lattice with a door in it. The children had thoughtlessly closed this door, and then, on starting away to play, had called and called to the dog to follow them. Poor little beast! He had hunted faithfully for an opening, had tried to fling himself bodily through the obstruction, and finally had attempted to dig a place beneath the lattice; but being a boy's dog and wildly impatient to follow his beloved companion, he had not dug deep enough, and in attempting to squeeze through, he had stuck fast. I ran frantically about, looking for some tool or implement that would be of service, and at last, with the aid of a fire shovel and much petting and soothing, I succeeded in digging him out; and the next moment he was sending a shower of gravel back from his flying feet as he tore off after his chums, Harry and little Sue.

Like most boys' dogs, Friday was a mongrel. It would be much easier to say what he was not than what he was, for he was neither retriever, pointer, St. Bernard, Newfoundland, bull, nor mastiff—nor anything else that was well-bred or clearly defined; but he was intelligence itself.

He was never tired, never cross; he was always ready to eat or sleep. He was of medium size, and he had a yellow-brown coat of short stiff hair marked by a dark stripe running down his backbone. Nature had carelessly given him four misfit feet much too large for him. At first sight people were apt to pity him for having to carry about such length and weight of caudal appendage as he had, and declared he should have been divorced from it in his earliest youth; but once they saw the very tempest of joy that lumpy long tail could express—saw it like a harp-string fairly vibrating with love and devotion—they felt there was not one inch too much of it. In his ridiculous body he showed all the flighty activity of a fox-terrier, while in his rare moments of quietude his face wore a truly mastifflike gravity.

On the morning of the equinoctial storm, two years before—a Friday morning—Mr. Ames, on opening his door, had found on the porch a wet, shivering, forlorn little puppy. He was empty, he was cold, and probably he was frightened, but he didn't show it if he was; on the contrary, he rose and ambled with shivery joy to meet Mr. Ames, to whose face he lifted his bright eyes, gazing at him with that expression of immeasurable, undying trust that is found in its perfection only in the eyes of a boy's dog.

Mr. Ames, as he stepped quickly back to avoid the rain, exclaimed, "Well, where on earth did you come from?"

But the puppy, moved doubtless by the same impulse to avoid further wetting, slipped inside without answering the question, and with the air of saying, "Yes, thank you, I *will* come in and rest awhile, since you press me so!" he ambled across the room toward the stove. But his muddy feet left a number of tracks on the creamy whiteness of the kitchen floor, and Mrs. Ames—bustling and indignant—was making some threats about "putting that horrid little beast right out of there!" when Harry came in. The moment the bold blue eyes of the boy met the brown bright eyes of the dog, they understood each other—each recognized in the other his missing chum.

"Oh, Mother!" cried Harry. "I want him!"

And Mrs. Ames, turning the pancakes with unnecessary emphasis, replied that he "might go right on wantin'! If he wanted a dog, he'd better wait and get a good one, not a poor, miserable, splay-footed, no-breed thing like that!"

"Oh, please, Mama, please let him stay just today, to play 'Man Friday' when I'm 'Robinson Crusoe'! See his nice footprints already made—and you won't let me go to school today—and I have to play with something!" and so on; and Mrs. Ames, vowing that "she would ne'er consent—consented," of course.

The little waif, with rare discretion, had meanwhile withdrawn to comparative seclusion behind the cozy kitchen stove, where the pleasant warmth was gradually subduing his convulsive shivers; and when Harry placed before him a dish of warm bread and milk, the hungry little chap cleaned the dish, and then, stretching himself out behind the stove, he slept like a small log until the children came from the dining room and called him to take his part in their production of the thrilling drama of *Robinson Crusoe*. But before beginning that, they had to perform the important duty of naming him; and considering the day of the week and the part he was to play for them, they thought that "Little Man Friday" would be a suitable name. Mrs. Ames, for different reasons, quite agreed with them, for she declared that Friday was the worst day of the week, and the puppy was the worst-looking specimen of doghood she had ever seen!—taking the sting off her words, however, by placing a basin of drinking water in the corner for him.

And Mr. Ames, as he flapped his umbrella open and shut two or three times—to make sure it would open quickly when he got outside in the pouring rain—nodded his head and said, "The name would fit the puppy like his skin!"

Whereupon Sue, who was an observant small person, excitedly informed him that "his skin didn't fit 'im at all, but hanged jus' loose all over 'im—mebbe it wasn't his skin, after all!"

And Mr. Ames laughed and said: "Well, he can't go out and change it in such a storm as this, so he'd better grow as fast as possible and fill it up—but the name is all right!"

And so the little wanderer and waif had suddenly found himself in possession of a local habitation and a name. While he was known as Little Man Friday to the children, to the neighbors he was known as "Little Friday Ames." He filled his skin nicely now. He was not fat, mind you—no boy's dog ever has time to get fat—but his skin had that looseness at the back of the neck necessary for Harry's lifting him.

His ears were a bit jagged on the edges in consequence of his too ready obedience to Harry's promiscuous "siccings." Man Friday was not heavy enough to be a successful

fighter—not strong enough; he almost always got whipped; but that made no difference to him. A "*s-s-sic*'em" to a dog is what a "dare" is to a boy, and being a boy's dog, Friday couldn't take a dare. And had Harry "sicced" him at a royal Bengal tiger, he would have done his loyal, idiotic little best to tackle the awful beast.

It was surprising, the amount of knowledge the dog had gained in two years. Every boy in the neighborhood knew he was worth his weight in gold as a finder of lost balls. He could carry canes and bring sticks out of the water. He walked on his hind legs, sat up badly, and smoked a pipe worse, and was a grateful dog that these three tricks were only required of him on wet Saturday afternoons.

The only time he had ever wished he were away was when a visitor was trying to teach him to hold a biscuit on his nose, and then toss it up at command, and catch it. That experience greatly reduced his regard for grown-up people. He was no respecter of persons. He would rush madly into any neighbor's cellar, and tear everything to pieces there, at a merely whispered: "Rats, Friday!"

One poor housekeeper once remarked that when he got among her barrels she might have thought, from the noise he made, that she was in a cooper shop.

Like all intelligent dogs, he could measure time very well. Every morning he escorted the children to the school-yard gate, there giving up to Sue the small bag containing the primer, slate, and apples that in those days were considered sufficient for the beginning of every young person's education. This surrender was, of course, not made peacefully— every boy's dog will understand that. Man Friday, when bidden to give up the bag, growled as savagely as a full mouth would permit, and quite properly jerked the bag away from the hand held out for it. A struggle always followed, in which some very dreadful blows had to be inflicted by Sue's chubby hands, while the delighted tots looking on screamed with glee: "Oh, he's goin' to bite! Yes, he is too—he's goin' to bite!"

And then the invincible Sue boldly seized upon the long tail, and Little Friday Ames dropped the bag to defend himself; while, with shrieks of triumph, the bag was snatched up, and his duty of amusing the children done, he turned and trotted home alone, wisely attending to any visiting of his own during that period of quiet.

Truth to tell, Man Friday had but few friends of his own race. Gentlemen's big, well-bred dogs looked down on him, while he simply hated ladies' dogs himself, declining any acquaintance with them. But he had one chum, another boy's dog, that he was really fond of. He lived in another ward and went to school there with his boy. He had started out meaning to be a bulldog. He knew every required "point"—all about the "breadth of head," "depth of nose-top," "underhung jaw," "bowed legs," and "stub tail"; but somehow or other he had been dipped into the wrong dye pot: he was perfectly black. Think of it!—he who was to have been pink of skin, white of coat, and with just a patch over his eye! This so rattled him that while he bowed his legs he got them much too long, which made him forget to push his nose up into his forehead. And the very first time he got a good look at himself, he said, he knew if he wasn't drowned he'd simply have to be a boy's dog; no one else on earth, it seemed, could look at him without laughing rudely or throwing stones at him—and every dog knows that the stones hurt the least.

But the day he was to have been drowned was so cold the water froze, and next morning he went out and hunted up a boy who was always fighting, and proved to him that, though his "points" were all wrong, he had the true bulldog grip and pluck; and his boy named him "Terror," which was shortened to Terry for everyday use.

And Terry, the black, long-legged, long-nosed freak of a bulldog was Little Man Friday's closest friend, and they often met at a German restaurant. They both were sober dogs, but this shop was midway between the two schools, and therefore convenient for both; and they could retire into the backyard and crawl under a grind-stone, and, in its cool shadow, discuss everything.

But never, *never,* even in Terry's company, did Little Man Friday fail to keep tab on the flying moments. Never once did the Comanche yell of the first boy out of school fail to be answered by the shrill *ki-yi, ki-yi!* of Little Friday Ames, who was outside the school-yard gate, ready for duty—for leaps over clasped hands, races, tearing imaginary game from the unwilling earth, or to fight anything he was sicced at.

Oh, yes, Friday could tell other hours besides meal times. What he didn't know about boys was certainly not worth knowing. He put no trust in the boy with a handful of string; and it was amusing to see how cleverly he jockeyed with that boy, always keeping a bit behind. He knew his long tail suggested all sorts of ideas to a boy with string. Then, too, whenever he came upon an old kettle or pot or pan, he sat down right there and then! No whistling, no knee-patting, no "old-manning" could make him rise until the boys had moved on a bit. He was not cross, only firm—*very* firm! Pleasantly but very solidly he sat down hard and fast to guard that long tail of his, tucked safely beneath him. You see, his memory was an excellent one. He could see that between a boy and a dog—even between a swimming and a whipping—there was a natural association of ideas, as the saying is; but he considered a dog's tail and a tin kettle as natural enemies.

On the day mentioned, after having released Man Friday from his painful and humiliating position, I returned to the kitchen and sat down to regain my breath, while Mrs. Ames, still vexed over her unjelled jelly, went about putting everything in the perfect order her soul loved. She had just announced to me that "we might as well go into the sitting-room now, and have a look at those patterns," when I heard the rattle of gravel flung from flying feet, and saw Man Friday tear around the house, up the porch steps, and into the kitchen, where he flung himself against Mrs. Ames with yelps such as I had never heard from him before; he seemed literally wild with excitement and fear—his eyes so widely strained that they showed the bloodshot whites, his body shivering, froth about his jaws! Mrs. Ames rushed toward the door, crying out: "He's mad—as sure's you're alive, he is!"

But I had risen, and, looking beyond Man Friday into space, an awful thought came to me: *The children!*

Friday gave another bound against her, then rushed out to the head of the steps. Looking back and seeing that he was not followed, he sat down suddenly, lifted his muzzle, and gave forth a long howl.

"Mercy me!" Mrs. Ames exclaimed. "The dog's alone!" and then she called loudly, "Harry! Harry! Susie! Sue!"

At these names Little Friday sprang down the steps and, barking furiously, rushed to the gate. Mrs. Ames staggered, and for one moment put her hand out and clung to the door, when Man Friday returned, caught her apron in his teeth, and, running backward, pulled her to the porch.

The next moment she and I rushed out, and the passersby saw two terrified women apparently playing tag with a common yellow dog in the public street; but then, appearances are very deceptive things sometimes.

We had not far to go, only to the next corner, and there Little Friday, after looking back to see if we followed, turned the corner. My brain was working fast. Where were the children likely to go in that street to play? Mr. Brown's private stable?—there was a pony there! No; Friday had passed Mr. Brown's house. To the lot where there was a house being built? Nothing could happen there; the men would see to that. The men? The *men*? Had I not heard that work had been stopped there for some days? Friday had turned in there, his spasmodic barkings telling *me,* at least, that he was digging. A mass of fallen sand at the foot of the little cliff—at one end a crowd of small footprints all pointing the same way, telling plainly of a childish stampede, Sue's little hat on the ground, and devoted, frantic Man Friday digging like mad!—that was what we saw when we turned into the open lot.

After that it seemed a sort of nightmare: the summoning of help, the digging, the cautions to be careful not to hurt the children with the shovels should they really be there, the prayers and sobs of Mrs. Ames; and through it all the panting breath of Little Man Friday digging, digging all the time! Then there was a cry from the mother. The dog had uncovered a bit of Sue's pink dress! Then, leaving *her* to stronger helpers, Friday turned away to win his final triumph! Looking at the digging men, a sort of pitying contempt came into his face, his manner saying as plain as day, *Oh, those men! Why don't they put their noses to the sand and find my boy's trail before they dig like this?* And suiting the action to his thought, he nosed along the sand, and then suddenly began a fierce digging at a spot quite removed from the men, while he barked with all the strength he had left!

"Oh," I cried, "see Little Man Friday! You are working in the wrong place—I am sure you are—Man Friday says so!"

The men looked up at one another. Every moment told: an instant wasted might mean life or death! Yet the dog seemed so sure he was on the right track that Little Man Friday was accepted at once as their guide, master workman, and boss; and where he led they *found*. Presently the rescued children lay upon the ground, their nearly suffocated little faces turned upward to the blessed light and air, while, whimpering and shivering, Man Friday ran from one to the other noisily barking his song of joy at their rescue.

When restoratives had been applied and the children removed to their home and put to bed, Harry called rather weakly, "Friday! Friday!" And at that call poor Friday simply lost his wits. He howled, he leaped, he barked, he chased his own tail round and round until he fell over, a helpless heap of joy!

* * * * *

As we sat at dinner that day, Mrs. Ames said in her determined manner:

"James, I want a piece of the *breast* of that chicken, and plenty of gravy too. And what is more, please put it on that gilt-edged plate."

And then she rose with her grimmest air, and, walking to the kitchen, she placed the plate before the surprised dog—who up to that time had eaten from a tin pie pan—and remarked: "The best I have is what you'll get, little man, the rest of your days!" and she stroked him kindly.

The china plate worried Friday a bit—it was so fine—so he carried all the pieces of chicken off and ate them from the zinc under the stove, and afterward attended rather gingerly to the gravy—which was really too good to be left; then, earnestly wishing to show his appreciation of her kindness, he went to the cellar for a while, and by and by came into the sitting-room, dirty, panting, and happy, to lay at her feet a large rat.

But even that—though it frightened her into shrieks—could not shake Mrs. Ames's new-found liking for the devoted dog, whose intelligence and love had, under Providence, saved her two children.

As she counted her silver spoons and forks into their basket, she said to me, "As long as I'm a livin' woman, I'll never say a word against stray dogs again; for I shall never forget that it was the luckiest day of my life that brought to our door Little Man Friday."

* * * * *

"Little Man Friday," by Clara Morris. Published in St. Nicholas, *January 1903. Original text owned by Joe Wheeler. Clara Morris (1848–1925), born in Toronto, Ontario, was an actress and author of such books as* A Silent Singer, Life on the Stage, *and* The New East Lynne.

OLAF AND THE LEMMINGS

Arthur Dillon

They were such little animals that it was hard for Olaf to envision the destruction that might lie in their wake.

But he was soon to find out!

* * * * *

One evening when Olaf and Hans were coming from the barn with the pails of milk, Olaf said, "Hans, see the crows flying back to Thorsberg across the fjord from Oester Fells. They go every morning and come back every night."

"They go to feed," said Hans, "and come back to roost in the Thorsberg fir-wood."

"They never did it before this winter," said Olaf. "They always flew up the fjord and then up the valleys to the grain stacks, all the way to Jornansstead and beyond. There's nothing for them to eat in Oester Fells."

"There must be," said Hans, "else why should they go? And see how strongly they fly; be sure they find enough."

"What is it?" asked Olaf.

"Go see," said Hans, "and don't stop to ask questions while the milk freezes." And with that they went on to the warm farmhouse.

Olaf liked nothing better than to "go see," especially if it was to go on the Oester

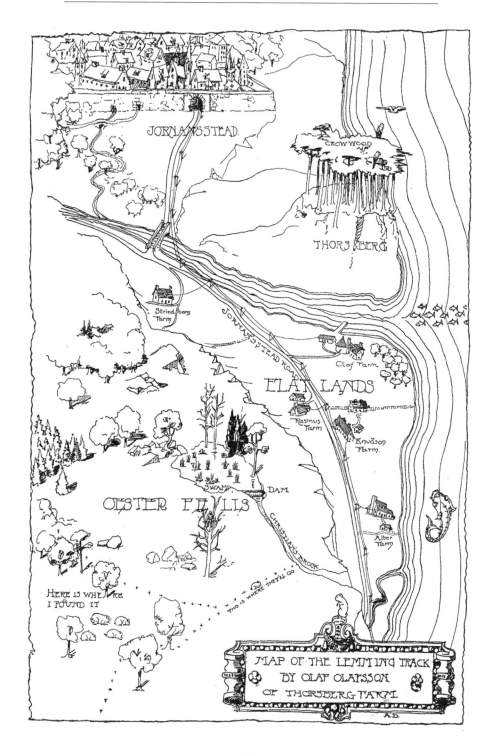

Fells, for they were a fine place in winter—a high, flat plain, twenty miles wide, with bunches of firs and pines scattered about, and now and then a hawk or the track of a fox or even of a wolf; and once the men of Jornansstead had killed a bear there in the snow. In summer the rocks and holes and high heather made it impossible to go across; but now it was one great sheet of snow, with big drifts piled against the trees, and long smooth hollows where the wind had swept the snow away.

So, early on the next morning, with a lunch in his pocket, Olaf set off on his skis.

It was hard to climb the steep slope that led up to the Fells from the flat farm-lands along the fjord, and Olaf had many a slip and tumble before he reached the top. There, if he had looked back, he could have seen the farmhouses and the barns like black spots on the snow far beneath him, and beyond, the sea, with perhaps some icebergs on it; but Olaf kept his eyes on the crows, for the last of them were disappearing ahead over the Fells.

The sun was bright and the wind was still, and he set out over the crust, his skis going *Squeak, squeak,* as he made long steps and pushed with his pole. Here and there, on the powdery snow that lay on the crust like sugar on a cake, he could see tracks of a hare or of a partridge; he did not turn aside to follow them but kept on, mile after mile, until the sun was high and he was hungry. He stopped in a clump of firs to eat his lunch, without having found where the crows had gone.

When he started on again, he saw, to his delight, a crow fly up ahead, and he ran forward quickly to the spot. A whole flock were there on the snow, and they rose, squawking, and settled on the trees to watch what Olaf would do. He looked about to see what they had been at, and went to and fro over the snow among their tracks, and at last found the body of a queer little animal such as he had never seen before. The crows had been pecking it, yet still he could see that it was like a fat rat, but with a rounder nose than a rat's, and round ears and a short tail, while its fur was a nice soft brown, mottled with darker spots. Then he saw that among the tracks of the crows' feet were many tracks such as the animal's little feet might have made; and in the distance more crows were flying about, rising up into the air and plunging down again, and seeming to be very busy over something. *More little animals,* Olaf thought. But it was growing late, and Olaf had far to go. It would not do to try to go down the slope from the Fells in the dark, as he would have to do if he lingered longer; besides, he was sure he knew what the crows came for, though he did not know its name, so, putting the little animal in his pocket, he set out for home.

Hans and his father were at the barn milking the cows when he came into the farmyard, holding his prize up by the tail for them to see. They both looked very grave over it.

"What is it?" asked Olaf.

"A lemming," said Hans.

"What's a lemming?" asked Olaf.

"A lemming is a traveling rat," said his father. "Where there is one, there are thousands. They come from no one knows where, nor why. They stop in the winter under the snow and live on moss and twigs and berries and on the bark of trees. They make long tunnels under the snow. The crows catch them when they come out to gnaw the firs by day; the foxes and wolves catch them by night. And the hawks catch them, and the sleet storms kill them, and the melting snow drowns them in the spring, but, in spite of all that, when summer comes there are thousands more than there were in the fall. And then, one night, they set off in a great army, straight ahead. Nothing stops them. They climb hills, they swim rivers, they gnaw through fences. When they come to a house, they pour into the windows at one side and out at the other. While some stop to devour, the others keep on, and when all have passed, nothing is left, nothing that they can gnaw or spoil. Even the farm stock has gone, for the frightened cattle run off."

"Will they come here?" asked Olaf.

"Who knows?" said his father. "They will come down from the Fells in the summer, and over someone's farm, ours or another's."

"If they cross the farms," said Olaf, "they will come either to the fjord or to the sea, and then they will have to come back."

"If they come to the sea, they will swim out and drown," said Hans. "If they come to the fjord, they will swim it, and cross Thorsberg and come to the sea beyond it. They always come to the sea at last and drown."

"Do they?" asked Olaf of his father.

"Yes," said his father, "but it is because they are obstinate and stupid. They will not turn aside. When they meet a river, they swim across; when they come to the sea, they try to swim across that, and so drown. Hans, can you make a long journey tonight?"

"Why not?" said Hans. "It is a long night."

"Olaf and I will see to the cattle. You take your skis and go to every farm that lies below the Fells and show the lemming. Then go to Jornansstead and show it to the mayor. One farmer out of every five must meet in the morning on the Oester Fells here above my farm, with the mayor and the public committee of Jornansstead. Show the lemming, and they will come. You need not come back till evening if you are tired."

"Tired!" said Hans. "The fat committeemen will be the tired ones, trying to keep up with me coming back. I will take Olaf's skis; they are lighter than mine."

That made Olaf feel proud, for he had made the skis himself, and Hans was a good judge of skis. He watched him glide away in the dusk and listened to the *squeak, squeak* of the skis on the snow long after Hans was lost to sight.

Olaf slept soundly in spite of dreams of countless brown rats, more soundly than the farmers whom Hans woke, battering on their doors and shouting, "Lemmings!" until they came with a light and saw for themselves. Later, his father awakened him in the dark, and they climbed up the slope to the Fells by the light of the setting moon. There already the farmers were gathering, and a little after daybreak Hans appeared with the burghers from Jornansstead; and, to Olaf's relief, with Olaf's skis, for he had had to use Hans's, which were heavy. They set off two by two, Olaf in the lead, guiding them along his tracks of the day before, with the mayor in his red scarf beside him.

When they came to the place where Olaf had found the lemming, they separated, some to the right, some to the left, some straight ahead, and explored the Fells for miles around. They gathered again for lunch and built a great fire, and while they sat around it and ate, with their skis stuck upright in the snow behind them, each told, in turn, what he had seen. It was all the same thing, lemming tracks, lemming burrows everywhere. When all had spoken, they discussed what to do, each man telling what he knew of lemmings. Then the mayor said, "The lemmings will not move far until the heather is in bloom. That we know. Let us watch them until then. Let us put marks on the trees around this land where they now are, and each week we will come to see if they have moved at all, and in what direction, toward whose farm."

Olaf's father said, "Let each pay a tax according to his farm, and let it be given to him whose farm is crossed, so that no one man shall be ruined."

"That is good," said all the farmers, and one said, "It will need someone to come each week to watch the marks."

The mayor said, "Let us appoint Olaf, Olaf's son. He has sharp eyes, and it will be an honor."

"That is good," said Hans, and all laughed, except Olaf, who tried not to look too well pleased. Then the farmers cut blazes on the trees with their hatchets, while Olaf watched the fire, until long after nightfall; and they all went home again, two by two, on their skis, in the moonlight, and Olaf was so sleepy that he never knew how he got down the slope of the Oester Fells, and into his bed, where he found himself the next morning.

Each week thereafter Olaf went over the Fells and visited the marks, and made new ones wherever he found the lemmings' tracks and burrows beyond the old ones. With his father's help he made a map (as you will see) showing just how the lemmings were shifting about. Soon it was plain that they were moving little by little to the east, and soon the outline of the marks on the map made like a tongue pointing to where the Fells came close to the sea, but still toward a good many farms. Olaf traveled again and again over ground between the lemmings and the edge of the Fells. He found that a line in the direction that the tongue pointed across Christian's Brook, that ran, in summer, from a low, swampy place on the Fells. He had an idea and told his father of it. Together with Hans, they went over the ground again and drew the brook and the swamp on the map, and Olaf's father took it all to the mayor. He called a meeting of the farmers, and they voted to adopt the plan Olaf's father had proposed.

Olaf watched the marks until the snow had melted away under the spring sun and rain. By that time the lemmings had moved to within a mile of Christian's Brook. After that there was no way to trace them, even if one could have gone to them through the high brush and the great stones the melting snow left bare. If one did not mind cold water, he could scramble up the bed of Christian's Brook from the ravine where it cut through the edge of the Fells clear to its head in the swamp. From there the farmers cut a rough road for half a mile toward the lemmings, and at the end of it built a platform in a high tree for a watchman. At the head of the brook, they built a long dam of stones and mud and bushes, so that the water was held back in the swamps and the brook ran nearly dry.

When the leaves were green, Olaf spent every day that he could leave the farm on the high platform. There, far up, he could see about him to the smoke of Jornansstead in the north, to the blue mountains to the west and to the south, and to the east over the sharp edge of the Fells to the sea. The crows of Thorsberg had broken up their winter flock and no longer flew over at dawn and back at night, but they came singly or in pairs, many of them at all times, plunging down to the Fells, and flying heavily away with young lemmings in their claws. The gyrfalcons and the hawks hovered thickly overhead, more than Olaf had ever seen before. Even the ospreys no longer soared over the sea, but they, too, sought their prey on the Fells; and at night one could hear the foxes barking in the heather.

Late one summer day the birds flew thicker than ever. Instead of being scattered all through the air over the Fells, they were gathered in a great cloud over the place where Olaf had put the last marks before the snow melted. He could hear their cries, and when Hans came to take his place and watch through the night, Olaf begged to stay, and he watched them soaring and swooping, coming and going, until the long dusk grew so dim he could see them no longer, and then he went to sleep.

He was awakened by Hans shaking him and shouting in his ear. With his eyes half open, he said crossly, "What's the use of shouting so? I'm as awake as you are."

"Are you?" said Hans. "That is good, for the lemmings have started at last. Listen. Look."

Sure enough, in the stillness of the early morning he could just hear a soft rustling and brushing in the heather and grasses, and innumerable faint squeaks seemed to arise from all about. It was still not light enough to see, but Olaf could not wait. He climbed down the rough ladder to the ground and ran with matches in his hand to set fire to the signal that had been made ready months before, a great pile of dry wood at the bottom of a pine tree. He tried to jump along from rock to rock, but once or twice when they were too far apart, he had to jump to the ground; and he then felt the lemmings scurrying past his feet, some of them stopping long enough to bite at his thick shoes. In a moment he had struck a match, and the signal was ablaze. The flames sprang up, and before he was back at the foot of the ladder, the whole pine tree was in flames like a great torch, with a high plume of smoke and sparks streaming straight up into the air. From Jornansstead, from the farms on the fjord, from Thorsberg, and all along the edge of the Fells, the answering fires flared up, showing to Olaf and Hans, as they raced over the rough road to the dam, that the farmers had been keeping faithful watch and had seen the signal. It was nearly clear daylight when they reached the dam. They were the first, but soon others came, and each took his appointed station, some at the gates of the dam, others scattered along the brook to where it ran over the edge of the Fells.

Soon one man set up a shout. Another took it up, and it was passed back from man to man to those at the dam, telling them that the first of the lemmings had reached the bed of the brook. They pulled up the gates, and the water sprang out. They broke down the dam with their poles and cleared a wide passage so that the water could run freely. It filled the bed of the brook with a racing, foaming torrent, so swift that some of the men were swept off their legs and went bumping over the rocks until they could right themselves and crawl out.

Olaf thought that such a river would soon drain the swamp dry, but one look at the great lake they had made by means of the dam reassured him, and he hastened off, with all the others, to where the lemmings' track met the course of the brook. All the farmers were gathered along one bank. Over the other, a brown stream of lemmings poured out of the bushes and into the torrent. There it disappeared. As fast as they came, just so fast were they carried away by the raging water. Not one could swim across, but all as soon as they touched the stream were swept down. And still they came, more and more of them, while the flood in the bed of the brook ran higher and higher and swifter and swifter. A few were tossed out on the bank far below, but there, too, the farmers were ready and pushed them back.

For two hours Olaf watched the steady, undiminishing procession coming over the opposite bank. Then, when he was commencing to wonder whether the swamp would not be drained dry before all the lemmings were drowned, the last of the swarm came over the bank and into the brook, and that was the end, like coming to the end of a long ribbon. The farmers gave a great shout. Not a lemming had escaped. All were washed down into the sea, and the seagulls and the ospreys and all the large fish of the coast gathered and ate them up.

* * * * *

There was a town meeting in Jornansstead that week. Olaf went with his father and listened while the pastor offered a prayer of thanks. Then the mayor arose and said, rapping first on the table, "Farmers of Jornansstead and Thorsberg Fjord, you have heard what our pastor has said. All of you agreed with him, for all of you saw the lemmings and all of you know what we have been spared. There was a great tax laid, and all of you have paid it willingly. But it has not been spent. A little was spent to build the dam, a little was spent to cut the road, a little to pay the watchers, and a little for the signal-fires. All of those littles added together made only another little, so that nearly all of the tax can be given back, and so it shall be. Is that good?"

"That is good," said all the farmers together. "Yes, yes, that is good!"

"But," said the mayor, "I have here a purse made of the skin of the first lemming that was found. Let us put some of the tax in it and give it to the one who found the lemmings, and who watched them so faithfully, and who thought of a way to kill them. So let us put enough in this purse to buy—"

"A gun—just a little one," said Olaf, nearly dancing in his seat.

"Be still," said his father. "You are rude."

But the mayor laughed, and all the farmers roared with laughter, and said, "That is good. Just a little gun," and laughed again.

And that is how Olaf got his gun.

* * * * *

"Olaf and the Lemmings," by Arthur Dillon. Published in St. Nicholas, *November 1910. Original text owned by Joe Wheeler. Arthur Dillon wrote for magazines early in the twentieth century.*

THE KITTEN AND THE BEAR

Charles D. Rhodes

* * * * *

Over a hundred years ago, when Yellowstone National Park was still administered by the U. S. military, this remarkable event took place, and was recorded for St. Nicholas *magazine by Lieutenant Rhodes in 1897.*

* * * * *

The safest place for the big game of this country at present is within the limits of the beautiful Yellowstone Park. Here, protected from the rifle of the hunter by two troops of United States cavalry, immense herds of elk, deer, and antelope wander about as securely as before the march of civilization reduced their feeding grounds to the wildest and most inaccessible parts of the great West. Here also the wilder animals—bears, panthers, and wolves—are protected by law, and have increased to such numbers as to be very much in evidence to dwellers in the park. Even a few buffalo, survivors of an almost extinct species, are seen now and then, their lives in constant peril, due to the high price paid at present for genuine buffalo robes.

Even with the aid of the troops, patrolling in summer and in winter on snowshoes, it is not possible entirely to prevent hunting. Poachers from the neighboring states, Wyoming, Idaho, and Montana, persist in defying the law and repeatedly attempt to elude the vigilance of the patrols. Thanks to recent severe laws, and to the admirable work of the superintendent of the park, poaching has almost ceased.

When the park shall be so enlarged as to include feeding grounds now outside its limits—grounds to which the grazing animals are prone to wander, then will this magnificent game preserve, this wonderland of nature, more nearly fulfill the purposes for which it was set aside.

Naturally enough, with no legal hunting permitted, all the game has become very tame. Herds of deer and elk come constantly near the little army post, Fort Yellowstone; and as for bears, they have become so fearless as actually to wander in and eat the scraps thrown out from the hotels. One big fellow invaded the camp of a cavalry troop a short time ago, thrust his huge claws through a wall tent containing the soldiers' beef ration, and was only driven away with a club wielded by the highly indignant troop cook. Even in this paradise for wild animals, the bears must be made to respect the laws against stealing.

It is about one particular black bear that I wish to tell.

Chris Burns, the veteran first sergeant of Troop D, had a kitten which, during the summer camping of the troop at the Lower Geyser Basin, made her home within the sergeant's tent. Here, curled up on a pair of army blankets, she defied the world in general, and dogs in particular. When the latter approached, she would elevate every bristle on her brave little back, her eyes would glow like live coals, and her tail would swell up threateningly. If dogs approached too near, she would hiss, and exhibit the usual signs of hostility, until the intruders had vanished from her neighborhood.

One day, when the camp was bathed in sunshine, and every soldier in camp felt lazy, an inquisitive black bear came down the mountainside, and, whether because he was in search of adventure or because attracted by a savory smell from the cook's fire, began to walk about among the white tents of the cavalry command.

Suddenly the kitten caught sight of him. Dogs by the score she had seen, but this particular "dog" was the largest and the hairiest dog she had ever seen. But she did not hesitate.

It was enough for her that an enemy had invaded her special domain. Hissing forth her spite, while her little body quivered with rage, she darted forth at the bear. The onslaught was sudden, and one glance was enough for Bruin. With a snort of fear, Bruin made for the nearest tree, a short distance away, and did not pause until he was safely perched among the upper branches! Meanwhile the kitten stalked proudly about on the ground beneath, keeping close guard over her huge captive, her back still curved into a bow, and her hair still bristling with righteous indignation, while her tail would now and then give a significant little wave, as if to say, "That's the way I settle impertinent bears."

The soldiers, who meanwhile had poured forth from their tents, could scarcely believe their eyes; but there was the bear in the tree, and the kitten below, and there were those who had seen the affair from beginning to end.

And perhaps the strangest part of it all was that the bear would not stir from his safe position in the branches until the kitten had been persuaded to leave her huge enemy a clear means of retreat! Then he slid shamefacedly down from his perch and ambled hastily off toward the mountains.

* * * * *

"The Kitten and the Bear," by Charles D. Rhodes. Published in St. Nicholas, *November 1897. Original text owned by Joe Wheeler. Charles D. Rhodes wrote for turn-of-the-twentieth-century magazines.*

OLD BALDY

Jack London

No one—make that no multiples of one—had ever been able to get the best of Old Baldy yet. That is why he changed hands so cheaply.

Then along came Deacon Barnes, as stubborn as the ox. However, in the showdown, all bets were on Old Baldy.

* * * * *

"I declare! So the deacon's goin' to try his hand on Old Baldy, eh?" Jim Wheeler chuckled gleefully at the news and rubbed his hands. "Waal, mebbe somethin' 'll happen," he went on, "an' mebbe it won't, but I sha'n't be a mite s'prised if Old Baldy come out a-top."

"The deacon's got a right powerful will," Sim Grimes suggested, dubiously. "An' so has Baldy—powerful'st will in the country, bar none. But critters is critters, and—" And Grimes was just preparing to unload his mind of certain ideas concerning man's primacy in the physical world, when the other cut him short.

"Now jest look here, Sim Grimes! Have you ever hearn tell of one man what limbered up Old Baldy when Old Baldy wa'n't so minded? There's Tucker an' Smith an' Johnson, an' Olsen, an' Ordway an' Wellman—didn't the whole caboodle try their luck at breakin' Old Baldy's sperrit, an' didn't the whole caboodle give it up? Jest tell me this, Sim Grimes—did you ever in yer born days hear of one man or passel of men gettin' Old Baldy on his feet when he took it into his head to lay down?"

"Mebbe yer right," Sim Grimes assented mildly, then his old faith in Deacon Barnes returning. "But the deacon's got a right powerful will." "But Deacon Barnes jined a Prevention of Cruelty to Animals society, didn't he?" Grimes nodded. "An' he don't b'lieve in whippin' dumb brutes?" "Nope." "Then how in the land of Goshen kin he make Old Baldy git up when he ain't in the mood?"

"It's more'n I kin tell," Grimes answered, at the same time starting up his horses. But before he was out of earshot, he turned and called back, "But the deacon's got a powerful will!"

The farmers of Selbyville had little use for Old Baldy, and less regard; yet he was one of the finest oxen in the country, and perhaps the largest in the state, says a writer in the *American Agriculturist*. A good worker and a splendid yoke-animal, a stranger might have wondered at the celerity with which his various owners rid themselves of him, after having been inveigled into buying him. The same stranger might have worked him a week before he discovered why, and again an hour would have sufficed to unearth the secret. Old Baldy had but one fault—he was stubborn. And he manifested this stubbornness in but one way. Whenever things did not exactly go to suit him, he simply lay down in his tracks, there and then, consulting neither his own nor his master's convenience. And there he would stay. Nothing could move him. Force was useless; persuasion as bad. The heavens might roll up as a scroll, or the stars fall from their seats in the sky, but there Old Baldy would stay until of his own free will he decided to get up and move along. Never from the time yoke was first put upon him had a man succeeded in budging him against his will. It was asserted that he had caused more gray hairs to grow in the heads of the Selbyville farmers than all the mortgages of the past three generations. He always went absurdly cheap, and man after man had bought him in the fond hope of conquering him, and winning not only the approbation of his fellows, but a very good bargain. And man after man had sold him for little or nothing, insanely happy at being rid of so much vexation of spirit.

"As stubborn as Old Baldy" became a figure of speech, the common property of the community. Fathers conjured obedience from their sons by its use; the schoolmaster employed it on his stiff-necked pupils; and even the minister calling sinners to repentance, blanched the cheek of the most unregenerate with its brand. But in the language of Deacon Barnes alone, it had no place. It was his wont to smile and chuckle when others made use of the phrase, till people remarked it would be a blessing if he only got the tough old ox once on his hands. And now, after Old Baldy had become thoroughly set in the iniquity of his ways, the deacon had bought him off Joe Westfield for a song. Selbyville looked forward to the struggle with great interest, and sly grins and open skepticism were the order of the day whenever the topic was mentioned. They knew the deacon had a will of iron, but they also knew Old Baldy; and their collective opinion was that the deacon, like everybody else who had tried their hand at it, was bound to get the worst of the bargain.

Deacon Barnes and Old Baldy were coming down the last furrow of the ten-acre patch back of the pasture. Five rods more of the plow, and it would be ready for the harrow. Old Baldy had been behaving splendidly, and the deacon was jubilant. Besides, Bob, his promising eldest-born, had just run halfway across the pasture and shouted that dinner was ready and waiting.

"Comin'!" he shouted back, no more dreaming that he would fail to reach the end of the furrow than that the dinner call was the trump of judgment. Just then Old Baldy stopped. The deacon looked surprised. Baldy sighed contentedly. "Get up!" he shouted, and Baldy, with a hurt expression on his bovine countenance, proceeded to lie down.

Deacon Barnes stepped around where he could look into his face and talked nicely to him, with persuasion and pathos mixed; for he feared greatly for Old Baldy's well-being. Not that he intended on whipping him brutally or anything like that, but—well, he was Deacon Barnes, with the ripened will of all the male Barnes that had gone before, and he hadn't the slightest intention of being beaten by a stubborn old ox. So they just looked each other in the eyes, he talking mildly and Baldy

listening with complacent interest, till Bob shouted a second time across the pasture that dinner was waiting.

"Look here, Baldy," the deacon said, rising to his feet, "if you want to lay there so mighty bad, 'tain't in me to stop you. Only I give you fair warnin'—the sweets of life do cloy, and you kin git too much of a good thing. Layin' down in the furrer ain't what it's cracked up to be, an' you'll git a-mighty sick of it before yer done with me." Baldy gazed at him with stolid impudence, saying as plainly as though he spoke, *Well, what are you going to do about it?*

But the deacon never lost his temper. "I'm goin' to git a bite to eat," he went on, turning away, "an' when I come back, I'll give you one more chance. But, mark my words, Baldy, it'll be yer last."

At the table, Deacon Barnes, instead of being at all irritated, radiated even more genially than was his wont, and this in the face of the fact that Mrs. Barnes had a mild attack of tantrums because he had kept dinner waiting. Afterwards, when he went out on the porch, he saw Jim Wheeler had pulled up his horses where he could look over the fence at the victorious Baldy. When he passed the house he waved his hand and smiled knowingly at the deacon, and went on to spread the news that the deacon and Old Baldy were "at it."

But there was a certain unusual exhilaration in the deacon's face and step as he led off to the barn with Bob following in his footsteps. There he proceeded to load up his eldest-born with numerous iron and wooden pegs and old pieces of chain and rope. Then, with his axe in hand, he headed back to the recalcitrant ox. "Come! Git up, Baldy!" he commanded. "It's high time we got this furrer finished."

Baldy regarded him passively, with half-veiled, lazy eyes. "Reckon it be more comfortable where you are, eh? B'lieve in takin' it easy, eh? All right. You can't say Deacon Barnes is a hard master." As he talked, he worked, driving pegs all about the stubborn animal. Then from the pegs he stretched the ropes and chains, passing them across Baldy till that worthy was hard and fast to mother earth—so hard and fast that it would have required a steam derrick to get him to his feet. "Jest enjoy yourself, Baldy," the deacon called, as he started away. "I'll come up to-morrer after breakfast an' see how you be."

True to his word, in the morning the deacon paid his promised visit. But Baldy was yet strong in his will, and he behaved sullenly as animals well know how. He even tried to let on that it was real nice lying out there with nothing to do, and that the deacon worried him with his chatter, and had better go away. But Deacon Barnes stayed a full quarter of an hour, talking pleasantly, with a cheery, whole-souled ring to his voice, which vexed Baldy greatly.

In the evening, after supper, he made another visit. Old Baldy was feeling stiff and sore from lying in the one position all day with the hot sun beating down upon him. He even betrayed anxiety and interest when he heard his master's steps approaching, and there was a certain softening and appeal in his eyes. But the deacon made out he didn't see it, and after talking nicely for a few minutes went home again. In the morning Baldy received another visit. By this time he was not only sore, but hungry and thirsty as well. He was no longer indifferent to his owner's presence, and he begged so eloquently with his eyes that the deacon was touched, but he hardened his heart and went back to the house again. He had made up his mind to do what all Selbyville during a number of years had failed to accomplish, and now that he had started he was going to do it thoroughly.

When he came out again after dinner, Baldy was abject in his humility. His pleading eyes followed his master about unceasingly, and once, when the deacon turned, as though to go away, he actually groaned. "Sweets do cloy, eh?" Deacon Barnes said, coming back. "Even lyin' in the furrer is vanity and vexation, eh? Well, I guess we'll finish this furrer now. What d'you say, Baldy? And after that you kin have somethin to eat an' a couple o' buckets of water. Eh? What d'you say?"

It can never be known for a fact as to whether Baldy understood his master's words or not, but he showed by his actions that he thoroughly understood his predicament.

"Kind o' cramped, eh?" the deacon remarked, as he helped him to his feet. "Well, g'long now, let's finish this furrer."

Baldy finished that furrow, and after that there was never a furrow he commenced that he did not finish. And as for lying down—well, he manifested a new kind of stubbornness. He couldn't be persuaded or bullied into lying down. No, sir, he wouldn't have it. He'd finish the furrow first, and all the furrows all day long. He grew real stubborn when it came to lying down. But the deacon didn't mind. And all Selbyville marveled, and a year afterward more than one farmer, including Jim Wheeler, was offering the deacon far more for Old Baldy than he had paid. But Deacon Barnes knew a bargain when he had got it, and he was just as stubborn in refusing to sell as Old Baldy was in refusing to lie down.

* * * * *

"Old Baldy," by Jack London. Published in Nor'-West Farmer, *February 5, 1900.*

MOONSHINE

Samuel Scoville Jr.

Have you ever wondered what could happen to your cat should, for one reason or another, the indoor "good life" disappear? Wonder no more, for that great nature writer, Samuel Scoville, tells the story of a cat that lived a Jekyll-Hyde life: lazy lounging house-life by day and feral tigerish-life by night. After reading this story, many readers will never look at a cat the same way again.

* * * * *

Moonshine was a spotted tabby. There are red tabbies and gray tabbies, both of which are striped like tigers. Moonshine, however, looked like a leopard, with her fur of yellow lake blotched with black, with curious overtones of saffron and orange-copper which at dusk merged into a glow of pale gold. She had a thick tail and pricked-up ears, while her pads and the tip of her nose were shrimp-pink and her eyes the color of amber, changing to emerald green at night. Like all tabbies, Moonshine numbered a bay lynx among her far-away ancestors, from whom she inherited her great size and weight—besides other characteristics not so apparent.

All that Betty Cassatt, her fifteen-year-old owner, knew of her pedigree was a single glimpse of Moonshine's mother. One winter afternoon in New York, as she reached the steps of her house on her way home from school, she saw a laughing crowd at a nearby corner held back by a huge policeman, while across the avenue,

with arched tail and head erect, in front of a tangle of traffic, paced a magnificent cat carrying in her mouth a tiny yellow kitten. Mrs. Cassatt had long been a patroness of the cat show, and Betty knew enough about cats to recognize the stranger as one of the "orange cats" that come from Venice, whither, in the days of the Doges, they had been brought from Egypt. This one might well have been the lineal descendant of Bouhaki, that proud cat who wore golden earrings and whose sculptured figure still sits at the stone feet of King Hana in dead Thebes. As Betty watched her, the great cat reached the sidewalk with her kitten still held in her mouth. Then, to Betty's surprise, she moved sedately up the steps and, dropping her baby at the girl's feet, vanished like a ghost.

From that day, Moonshine, as the foundling had been named, became one of the best-loved of Betty's many pets up at Runaway, Colonel Cassatt's country house in the Berkshires. From a fuzzy little ball of gold, she grew into a magnificent cat. Only in temperament did her mistress consider her to be lacking.

"She's too amiable and lazy to be interesting," Betty confided to her father one day in early October when the air tasted of frost. "All she cares for is to be comfortable."

"I'm not so sure," said the colonel, looking long into Moonshine's half-shut, golden eyes with the green gleam in their depths. "She may surprise us yet. Sometimes these sleepy-looking people are great adventurers at heart."

"No fear!" returned Betty, a little scornfully. "Moonshine spends most of her time sleeping on this veranda, and her idea of a great adventure is to parade once across the lawn and back. If you aren't careful, old dear," she went on, stroking the great cat's silky frill until she purred drowsily, "you'll get so fat and puffy that you won't be able to walk at all."

As they talked, the sun went down in a smoke of crimson and gold. Beyond the stone gates of the outer wall the tawny pink poverty-grass rippled down the bare slope to the edge of Blacksnake Swamp. On the crest of the Cobble, the sugar maples showed peach red and yellow ocher; the white ashes, vinous purple; the birches, honey yellow; while on the lower slopes, the staghorn sumacs were old-gold and dragon's-blood red. Under the frost, even the leaves of the common pokeberry showed carmine purple above and Tyrian rose beneath, and the cat-brier wore pure scarlet.

As the rim of the sun touched the horizon, there sounded from above, like drops of molten silver, the contralto sky-notes of bluebirds flocking for their journey southward. The thickets were full of the clicking notes of juncos and the flutter of their white skirts; while here and there, veeries flitted through the woods like tawny shadows. A wood frog sounded his fall note and a single white tree cricket chirped, the last of a vast chorus. Then from the woods came that saddest of all bird-notes, the wail of a screech-owl, like the cry of a little lost child. Betty shivered suddenly.

"Let's have Sasaki make a fire in the living room," she said, starting up suddenly. "Moonshine, you big lazy thing, come in where it's warm."

The great cat blinked sleepily and dropped her head on her forepaws.

"Sleep there, then!" said her mistress, a little petulantly. "That's all your life is, anyway—sleeping and eating."

One by one the stars of autumn shone out, ice-blue Vega of the Lyre, white Altair, between her guard stars, Algol, the demon star, and a myriad of others flamed and flared in the black-violet sky. As the hours passed, the fires in hall and living room died down. One by one, lights showed for a time in the upper windows and then went out. A wind of the night rattled the blinds and was gone, while, in the stillness of the dark, through quiet meadows and under silent trees, a tide of life ebbed and flowed and passed, as the wild-folk came out to live and love and die in this their day.

In the very mid of the night, Moonshine awoke and, in another second, was standing in the starlight, a very different animal from the one who had slept all day, curled up in a golden ball in the rocking chair. Vibrant with fierce life, she stretched and tested every muscle in her lithe, strong body, and unsheathed and sank one set after another of curved, keen claws deep into the rag rug, while steel-strong muscles writhed like snakes under her silken skin and her wide-open eyes burned like green flame. Then, with a bound, she leaped from the floor to the edge of an oak settle that stood near the outer door of the porch. Walking along its back until she reached the door, she stretched out at full length until both her padded fore paws rested on the knob of the door, and, pushing with one paw and pulling with the other, she turned the knob as quickly and quietly as any human could have done.

A moment later she was racing down the long slope of the lawn in a series of swift bounds. As the great cat reached the center of the lawn, she almost ran into a chestnut-brown animal, with gray-brown cheeks, which measured a good two feet from the tip of its snubby nose to the end of its flattened, naked tail, the hallmark of the muskrat, the largest of all the rat-people. This one, a mile from water, was a fierce old male, on one of those strange pilgrimages across country which muskrats often make by night in the autumn. On such excursions they will attack anyone they meet, man or beast, and no ordinary cat will risk an encounter with such a desperate fighter.

Moonshine, however, was not an ordinary cat. As the great rat rushed at her with a snarling squeal, she sprang straight up a full three feet from the ground and, whirling in midair, landed crouched on her opponent's back, where she drove crooked claws through the glossy fur and sank her four white daggers deep into its neck. Against such an attack, the muskrat struggled and snapped in vain. In another minute, the deadly teeth of the cat had pierced its spinal cord and the last battle of the old fighter was over. With hungry growls, under the midnight sky, Moonshine fed full on the rich dark meat of her kill, and the taste of blood seemed to make her even more a fierce, vibrant creature of the night.

Out through the great stone gates and across the pasture beyond she flashed, until she checked her stride at the edge of the woods, where a mist rose to meet her like a ghost. As always, the woods seemed to be waiting, and Moonshine knew that much might happen in that forest which stretched clear to the top of Rattlesnake Mountain, a long five miles away. Stealthily, craftily, she crept without a sound along a tiny trail, winnowing the air before her through the mesh of her wonderful nostrils which, for the wild-folk, are eyes and ears combined. Once she stepped aside and waited while a sniffing black-and-white figure, with a magnificent pompom of a tail, waddled past. Long ago Moonshine had learned that the unhasting skunk always has the right of way. Deeper in the woods, the path skirted the bank of a stream which flowed through a tracery of deep lavender shadows and showed all dusky silver against black masses of hemlocks.

Suddenly, from the dead top of a blighted chestnut, came a dreadful voice. *"Whoo, hoo-hoo, hoo, hoo!"* it sounded, and a black shadow drifted down toward Moonshine, from the midst of which, like orange fire, gleamed the eyes of that death-in-the-dark, the great horned owl. A second later that owl had the surprise of his long and blood-stained life. House cats who strayed into the woods by night, according to his simple creed, were lawful and easy prey. Yet as he swooped down upon this one, it flashed out from under his clutching talons, twice as large as any tame cat had any right to be, and, springing into the air with a snarl of fury, ripped his padded sides with lightning claws and just missed securing a death grip in the flesh beneath. Snapping his beak like a pistol shot, the great owl glided indignantly away, while Moonshine, her white teeth showing in the starlight, gazed after him as she rubbed clinging bits of down off her pink pads.

Well up the mountainside, cunningly hidden among the roots of a great beech tree, was a dry, roomy burrow lined with soft grass. Moonshine had a reason for reaching that burrow as rapidly as possible. To be exact, there were two reasons, soft, warm, fuzzy ones, with reddish-gray fur, all marbled with gold blotches. All day long these children of the wild had slept, rolled up in round balls of fur, but now they were waiting impatiently for their mother and their dinner. Wherefore Moonshine sped along the trail as fast as the rule of the forest would allow. Safety first is the law of long life among the wild folk, as among their human brethren, and one who hurries through the woods without taking time to heed the messages which the wind brings is apt to stop living abruptly.

Suddenly, something appeared in the trail ahead which stung the hastening mother into a burst of frantic speed. It seemed nothing more alarming than the print of two tiny, bare, baby feet. Yet even before she sighted them, her instantaneous nostrils had told her that those prints had been made by a raccoon, whose hind-paw tracks imitate his flat-footed cousin, the bear. Disregarding any possible prowlers of the night, or the traps which humankind are apt to sow along game trails, the great cat raced like a mad thing under the silent stars, and her lithe form, luminous in the dark as a will-o'-the-wisp, reached the burrow almost as soon as the old raccoon, who had been hunting leisurely ahead of her—almost, but not quite.

Akin to the bear, a raccoon also shows in his funny, foxy face that he is related to those great weasels, the martin, the wolverine, and the fisher, and, when occasion offers, the blood of the weasel-folk shows in his strange, blended nature. Tonight, the nostrils of this one told him that such an occasion was at hand, and just as Moonshine arrived, he had entered the short tunnel which led to the burrow among the beech roots. Only the blood and breeding of the two kittens within saved their lives. They had never been out under the sky, nor, indeed, had their eyes been opened for long, yet an infallible instinct told them that death was at their door. Another instinct, equally deep and inherited from fierce and grim ancestors on both sides of their house, roused them to meet death fighting. As the raccoon thrust its way into the burrow, the soft fur on the back of each kitten stood up, their tiny ears flattened, their short tails puffed, and with fierce little snarls, they both clawed with all their small might at the sniffing, pointed muzzle before them. Not expecting any such reception, the raccoon drew back.

Just as he was about to return, he heard in the distance, like an echo to the kittens' growls, a snarling screech of concentrated rage. In a second it had risen in a shrill crescendo as, with the swift and terrible rush of the cat folk, the maddened mother neared the den. The raccoon is among the wisest of the wild folk, and this one showed his wisdom by backing out of that burrow with a speed which one who had seen him enter would never have suspected that he possessed. The raccoon is a willing fighter, cool and fierce and stubborn, but he always prefers to fight in the open rather than in a cramped burrow. Quick as this one had been, he was none too quick. Even as he reached the outer air, a mottled, gold-yellow fury flashed at him. There are only two or three of the wild folk who care to risk a battle with a full-grown raccoon. The sight of this one, however, coming out from her burrow, maddened Moonshine beyond even the thought of fear, and a hot tide of mingled love and rage swept away every thought from her fierce brain except to save her kittens, or, if she had come too late, to kill their killer.

Ten feet away, she launched herself through the air like a leopard, trying, as would that far-away ancestor, for the back grip of her tribe. So sudden and swift was her spring, that few of the wild folk could have avoided it. The raccoon, however, was one of those few. Perfectly balanced on all four feet, he shifted, and slipped her lead, like the trained boxer that he was, so that the pounce of those armed paws missed him by an inch, and the cat landed by his side instead of on his back. That inch was as good as a mile to the raccoon. There was a flash of his fore paw, which looked curiously like a tiny human hand, save for the sharp claws, and immediately a long crimson weal showed the length of Moonshine's side.

Bounding like a ball, the great cat sprang again at the raccoon; but again he was not there, and once more she received another stringing slash which ran the whole length of her back. Fighting for any lesser stake, she might have retreated from the cool and deadly counters of her imperturbable opponent, yet that night she never even felt the pain of her wounds. Once more she rushed, this time herself striking a double blow with both paws quite as swiftly as the raccoon had done, and with far keener and deadlier claws. The raccoon sidestepped one slash, but the other landed. For a second, all five claws of the cat's left fore paw clutched deep in the loose grizzled fur.

It was enough. With the speed of light, Moonshine rushed into the clinch for which she had been striving, sank another sicklelike set of talons in the raccoon's back, and tried with all her teeth for the fatal throat hold. The gray fighter dropped his head, and two sets of fierce teeth snicked harmlessly against each other, while, with human hands and beast claws, he gripped her throat chokingly. Tooth for tooth, the fight was an even one, and although the crooked claws of the cat were sunk deep into the raccoon's back and shoulder, yet his were fixed in a punishing grip on her throat.

Then it was that Moonshine brought to bear the last terrible resort of her family. While the raccoon stood flat on the soles of his wedge-shaped hind feet, the cat swung her weight clear from the ground and delivered an eviscerating double slash with her raking hind claws. It was well for the coon that he wore loose, shaggy fur and was able, even in the clinch, to swing his unprotected breast slightly to one side, or the fight would have ended then and there as far as he was concerned. As it was, those ten crooked scimitars played havoc even with his tough body. *Churring* deep

5—STS

in his throat, he braced his human hands against the golden body before him and, twisting mightily, broke clear from the clinch. For a second, panting, bleeding, the two fighters faced each other. Suddenly, from the burrow beyond, there sounded two plaintive meows. They were not loud, but they meant more to Moonshine than any other sound on earth, for they told her that both of her kittens were unharmed and—hungry. Involuntarily she turned toward them.

The raccoon was perfectly willing to call the battle a draw. There was plenty of food in the woods, and it was clear to his cool brain that a pair of kittens was not worth a fight to the death. Accordingly, looking very fierce and growling deep to indicate what terrible things he would have done if the fight had gone on, he lurched into a nearby thicket. Not until he was out of sight did Moonshine enter her burrow. There she cuddled and nursed and licked her babies, and, like human mothers, doubtless decided that they were the most wonderful in the world. Then, rolled up in a round, warm ball, all three slept out the rest of the night.

At daybreak she dressed her wounds and made her toilet and that of her kittens—all with that pink, swift tongue which the cat folk use for comb, brush, sponge, and salve. When the sun was well up and all prowlers of the night had gone back to bed, she led her family away from their birthplace, never to return. That morning the Cassatts heard a loud mew at the veranda door.

"That's lazy old Moonshine," said Betty. "All night long she's slept in her chair. Now she'll drink her milk and go to bed again."

As the colonel opened the door, in marched Moonshine, sleek, imperturbable, with half-shut, golden eyes, purring as she came. Close behind her moved side by side two gray kittens, marbled and flecked with red and gold. As Colonel Cassatt stared at them incredulously, he saw that they had tiny pricked-up ears, that their tails were short, with broken black barrings and white tips, and that, instead of mewing, they growled deep in their little throats, standing stiffly and sternly the while on outspread legs.

"I told you Moonshine would surprise us yet," he remarked to Betty, as he bent down to examine the new arrivals. "Those kittens of hers are of the wildcat breed, and Moonshine must have brought them up clear over on Rattlesnake Mountain. No wonder she used to sleep all day. It looks, too, as if last night," he went on, examining the long raw furrows down her sleek sides, "she had put up a tremendous fight for her babies."

Betty knelt down and put her arms around the great cat's lithe body and looked long into her half-closed, inscrutable eyes.

"I apologize, you deceitful old darling," she whispered.

* * * * *

"Moonshine," by Samuel Scoville Jr. Published in St. Nicholas, *October 1923. Original text owned by Joe Wheeler. Samuel Scoville (1872–1950), naturalist and author, was one of the most prolific authors of his time.*

"Fancy! A Cow!"

Catherine R. Britton

They were all mixed in together—Peter Murphy and scholarships and wild-eyed cows and Shakespeare.

* * * * *

Have you ever crawled out of bed at 4:00 A.M., donned clothes so icy they seemed brittle, and stepped forth into a thirty-below morning to milk six cows—one of them being Lucretia? If you haven't, you'll never know what I underwent in an effort to better myself.

Mother and Dad went South that winter for Dad's health, so Bill and I were left to take care of the farm. Dad had insisted to the last minute, "And don't think of changing your plans, Kit. You start in at college just the same."

But when Mother was alone with us, she looked worried. "We can't afford to let you stay in town, Christine," she said. "And Bill needs the car out here. Perhaps you can arrange it so he can take you in mornings and go after you when you're through."

So we left it like that until the folks were gone . Then we sat down to figure things out.

"Don't see how I can do it, Kit," he began. My heart fell. Going on to college that year meant so much to me! Suddenly he raised his head and grinned engagingly. "Tell you what, Sis. Here's a bargain. If you'll do all the milking, I'll be able to take time off to drive you in. How about it?" He was only teasing, but I grasped at the straw.

"Do you mean it, Bill? Truly?"

But even as my spirits soared, I knew there was a catch to it. I knew by the jaunty way Bill strutted off. He was enjoying a joke all by himself.

* * * * *

That night I began my task. I was gone from the house five minutes when I marched out of the barn to accost Bill coming across the field.

"Bill Tolliver!" I demanded. "What in our barn is black and white and has the gentle ways of a cyclone?"

He grinned. "It must be Lucretia!" he announced.

"And Lucretia is—?"

"The cow Dad traded our old separator for. Are you ready to give up?"

"Give up!" My eyes must have flashed sparks at him, the way I felt. "No, Mr. Smarty. I'm going to college this year, and you're going to take me."

"Then milk Lucretia!" he chortled after me as I stalked away.

Well, I did. I spent half an hour getting a halter around her neck and hobbling her. Then I milked her, and it was pitch dark before I started on the other five cows.

But Bill is as good as his word. The next morning, after I had once more conquered Lucretia, the cow, he took me to town to register.

I came away happy. I had a perfectly grand course lined up. Besides the regular freshman subjects, I managed to get into a Shakespeare course.

Every morning, thereafter, found me up long before the sun, milking cows—and Lucretia. I refused to class that wild-eyed beast with the gentle animals who stood around as cows should and cast grateful eyes on me when I approached with a milk pail. Evenings it was the same way. A struggle with Lucretia, then the rest of the milking.

And the Shakespeare course promised to finish the little patience that Lucretia spared me. Professor Digby was a learned soul whose tongue was double-edged with sarcasm. The second day of school he asked me a question, and, reddening, I was forced to stammer out, "I d-don't know!"

He smiled cruelly. "Well!" he exclaimed with gentle emphasis. "You are about to find out."

But Speech Club, which I joined immediately, offered atonement for everything else. At one of the first meetings, Miss Renard announced the Alaire scholarship offered to the student giving the most outstanding interpretation of a Shakespearean passage.

My heart vowed, secretly, that I would give everyone a run for the scholarship, if I got a chance.

* * * * *

I don't know when Peter Murphy, son of the president of the college, first entered the picture. Looking back, I can see his mocking face everywhere: around the building—devoid of other young men, since it was a women's school; and always at those parties to which we were allowed to invite boys. He had gone to State for two years, but for some reason—health was the one given—he was at home this year.

Worn out as I was much of the time by Lucretia and Shakespeare, I was wont to snap at his lazy jokes. Instead of making him leave me alone, this seemed to give him greater delight in hanging around.

One night, decked in overalls, I was pursuing Lucretia around the yard, and she was eluding me quite capably, when I heard a hearty laugh. I looked up, and there stood Peter Murphy, leaning on a fence post. It was then that he made the remark which stung so deeply.

"Well! Cows! Imagine!"

He had brought me some material from Miss Renard—and he had come, of course, at such a time!

* * * * *

But outside of small disagreements, the situation was becoming serious for me. I was too tired at night to study much, and my course was heavy. So one morning early in November I took a copy of Hamlet's soliloquy and my lantern and milk pails out to the barn. The soliloquy must be learned, and there was no other time for me to do it.

I stuck it on the nail beside one of the stalls, held up my lantern now and then to read it, and memorized it, several lines at a time. By the time I had milked four cows, I knew it all. So on the fifth (the sixth being Lucretia) I practiced reciting it aloud. Lucretia stood near at hand, stamping her feet, rolling her eyes, and fairly daring me to come near enough to put the halter and hobbles on her.

"To be, or not to be," I chanted. I went on, milking frantically all the time.

Suddenly it seemed quiet. I looked up. There, watching me, not moving, stood

Lucretia. If a cow could be spellbound, I would say that she was just that. Her tail, instead of whipping frantically as was her custom, moved rhythmically back and forth. She chewed gently on her cud, and her eyes were calm.

"Well, for the love of Pete!" I burst out, staring back at her. "I've heard that music could do it—but I never imagined Shakespeare could have such effect—and on a cow!"

"It's a fight to the finish this time, Madam Lucretia," I said between my teeth. Seeing the stool and pail in my hands, she began her semi-daily contortions.

Above her racket I began to drone: "To be, or not to be-e-e—"

She quivered, then kicked at the pail. I pulled it away to safety and went on. "That is the question—"

It was working! With her head turned to watch me inquisitively, she stood while I settled the stool in place.

I patted her soothingly down through "to die—to sleep—"

Then I began to milk, chanting all the time.

I got stuck and had to go over it again. I didn't dare get up and look at the paper. But the second time through I remembered the ending. And, just as I rose triumphant, my pail of milk intact and myself still sound, I slapped her on the flank and cried out: "Thus conscience doth make cowards of us all!"

Lucretia, the unmanageable, almost smiled at me as she ambled off to join the herd in the feed yard.

I scarcely dared to hope that it would work again. But it did! All I had to do to make Lucretia stand docile and serene was to repeat Hamlet's lament. As a sort of game, I saved the last part, "Thus conscience doth make cowards of us all," as our parting cue: and within two weeks she needed only that, not the accompanying slap, to make her leave the stall.

By Christmas vacation, I was actually fond of the fiery-eyed little beast. What was more, I could sleep half an hour later in the morning, and I could depend on getting the milking done before supper at night.

* * * * *

In late March Shakespeare set his fangs upon me in dead earnest. We were to enact *Hamlet*! And what was my surprise to hear Prof. Digby tell us that, since Miss Christine Tolliver was the most ardent student in the class, she would play Hamlet.

Of course, it would be very amateurish, with only girls to play the parts, but it would be fun. And here was my chance to work for the scholarship!

As the night of the performance drew near, I began to lose all hope of that scholarship. Hamlet's soliloquy never went right.

"You know, you're not reciting to a kindergarten, Miss Tolliver," Prof. Digby said with biting irony. "Make it *real*."

Real! When to me it was nothing more or less than a cow call! But I did my best.

I had to stay in town all afternoon the day of the play; so I called Bill not to come after me, and Peter Murphy drove me home. Bill had promised to milk for me, and it would save him a lot of time if he didn't have to make an extra trip to town.

But I got home to find a note on the table:

Gone to help Dick. His horse is sick. You'll have to milk, Sis—I'm sorry. I left the car for you. Good luck.

* * * * *

It was five already. I went out to milk, and was almost through when I missed Lucretia.

No Lucretia in the feed yard, the barn, anywhere! A broken fence told the story. Lucretia was out, Bill was gone; so it rested with me to find her.

I saddled the only horse in the barn, Jerry, a plow horse with big feet and an immense back. And I started out.

I found her trail down the creek, and an open gate farther on guided me. The sun warned me that it was past six. I was hungry; I was tired.

Much later I saw Lucretia. She was nibbling grass at the side of the road, with little concern for the world of drama. And I realized with a sinking heart that it was too late to take her home.

So the hero of *Hamlet* joggled into town dressed in muddy overalls, riding a work horse, and driving before her a frisky cow.

The school was at the edge of town, so I drove Lucretia up to a lonely spot and tethered her to a fence, using the rope that we always kept on the saddle. I was about to rush away when I remembered that Lucretia hadn't been milked yet.

"She doesn't deserve to be!" I cried. Then, pitying the poor beast, I stooped over and started to milk Lucretia just enough to relieve the load in her bag.

A chuckle told me someone was witnessing the ridiculous scene, and the voice told me who it was.

"Hamlet!" exclaimed Peter Murphy.

"Hamlet" stood up in her muddy overalls. "Peter Murphy!" I said between my teeth. "If you ever mention this to me!"

He bowed low. "Never, I promise, will a word from me remind you of it." He grinned broadly and proffered his arm. "Shall we go?"

Red-faced, I marched by his side toward the auditorium. He chattered the whole way, but I could not forget my outfit, nor that ridiculous scene with Lucretia.

Everything went well that evening. I thrilled to the part of Hamlet, and I began to think that maybe I had a chance—just a wee one—to win that scholarship! If only I could make the soliloquy go right.

Act three began. I stood off stage, waiting for the king and Ophelia to lay their plans. And suddenly, all lights went out for me. Looking across the stage, I saw—oh! Unbelievable!—Lucretia, the cow—standing with her front feet on the step which led from the wings onto the stage. Behind her, flashing a grin at me, then vanishing, was Peter Murphy.

Lucretia's eyes rolled. What could I do! No one was there at the moment, and in a second the play would be ruined.

Someone pushed me forward. I went onto the stage, eyeing Lucretia, who could not yet be seen by the audience. I wondered what I should say.

"To be—" someone prompted hoarsely. Of course! And I began.

"To be, or not to be; that is the question—"

The rolling of Lucretia's eyes slowed from one hundred to twenty revolutions per minute. I went on.

If Hamlet was perturbed when he uttered his famous soliloquy, then I was desperate. I saw the janitor come up, tug at the rope around her neck. She wouldn't budge. I went on, and on—and at last I declaimed, "Thus conscience doth make cowards of us all."

Without more ado, Lucretia turned, following the guiding hand of the astonished janitor, and was seen no more by Hamlet.

When it was all over, I sat down on a chair, completely overcome.

"They want you out front, Kit."

In a dream, I went forward unsuspectingly, to hear President Murphy recite queer words.

"Christine Tolliver—superior performance—*Hamlet*—" the words came to me in loose sequence—"scholarship—" I took something and told him, "Thank you."

But as he went on, it burst over me what it was really about. "I want to congratulate you, especially, on your splendid interpretation of Hamlet's soliloquy."

I wanted to laugh out loud; I only nodded politely as I made my escape.

Peter Murphy, not smiling now, met me as I started to the dressing room. "The janitor has already started with Lucretia, and if you want to go home, you can use my car." Then he added, "You're game!"

Late that night, Peter Murphy took me home in his new roadster. At our gate, we stopped.

"I just want to tell you, Kit Tolliver—" he paused, "that I'm through being good-for-nothing. I'm going back to State next year and make good."

Before I could answer, the night was cut by a long-drawn— *"Moo-oo-oo!"*

We laughed. "Fancy! A cow!" I said.

* * * * *

"Fancy! A Cow!" by Catherine R. Britton. Published in The Girls' *Companion, March 27, 1938. Original text owned by Joe Wheeler. Printed by permission of Joe Wheeler (P.O. Box 1246, Conifer, CO 80433), and David C. Cook, Inc., Colorado Springs, CO 80918. Catherine R. Britton wrote for magazines during the middle of the twentieth century.*

THE TOUR OF THE FOUR

Abbie Farwell Brown

It was a most unlikely combination: a rapidly rising young reporter, a very pretty girl, two unmanageable and ungrateful cats, and a streetcar full of chuckling observers. But the story didn't end there.

* * * * *

Life and relationships were a lot more formal back when this story was first published in 1898—but, as you will see, they didn't stay that way!

* * * * *

It was Saturday afternoon, and I was off duty for the rest of the day, for I had been at work until three that morning, reporting a smash-up on the P. & O. Railroad. I had pleased the managing editor by making a scoop of important news by interviewing a prominent politician whom I had discovered badly damaged, but believing himself *incog* in an ambulance near the wreck, and of whom, by Napoleonic stratagem, I had secured an exclusive description of the whole affair. Hence my ticket of leave until Sunday morning.

I was now on my way, in a Brookton electric car, to make a long-delayed call upon a distant aunt—no favorite of mine—who I knew must be pining for my society. I had taken the only vacant seat in the car, opposite a very pretty girl who held a huge box in her lap, while another occupied the space beside her. She had cast a quick glance at me when I entered, as if she thought she knew me, and indeed there was something familiar about her own face; but I was at a loss to place it.

She was a stunningly stylish girl, and the enormous pasteboard boxes—unmarked and unremarkable—which obviously held neither candy nor millinery—did not at all harmonize with her neat tailor-made rig. Of this she tried to appear serenely unconscious, as well as of the fact that everyone was looking at her, and she really did it very well. The boxes were lashed and knotted carefully in every direction with stout twine; moreover, the covers and the sides were punched full of good sized holes, and at last it dawned upon my sluggish mind that there must be something alive inside.

Hardly had I reached this astute decision, when a prolonged and mournful *maiou* from the box beside her betrayed its correctness. The whole car began to smile broadly, and the girl's cheeks flushed, but her lips twitched on the verge of laughter as she bent over the box and appeared to whisper words of comfort through the cover. Just then a loud scratching and a strange bulging of the other box distracted her attention, and then began a duet of answering howls and caterwaulings fairly fiendish to hear.

Looking up quickly, her eyes met mine, and she could not resist a merry smile, which showed a row of the whitest teeth in the world. There was, indeed, something very familiar about that smile, and I know I must have stared unconscionably trying to remember where I had seen it, for, with a blush, she dropped her eyes again to her now wondrously quaking boxes. Each seemed animated by a small earthquake, which bulged and billowed the pasteboard surfaces into the most surprising curves and corners.

She did not soon look up again, though I continued to stare at her, wondering where I had seen that face before. Then, on the outskirts of Brookton the car stopped to admit a lady, for whom the girl hastened to make room by hastily lifting the heavy box beside her onto the other in her lap. I jumped up to offer the newcomer my own seat, but it was too late. The box came down with a dull thud, and a sound of rending pasteboard. There was a sudden frantic *ya-owl,* and through the side of the lower box was thrust a choking black head with bulging yellow eyes. The sudden movement of its prison cell had also greatly disturbed the occupant of the upper box, and with wild kickings and scratching, a corner of the cover was unexpectedly loosened, and another head, abject and gray, was protruded.

With a little exclamation of horror, the girl clapped a hand over each furry head

and tried to force them back. Several of us sprang at once to her assistance, with imminent danger of choking both cats, but among us all we succeeded only in increasing their struggles, to the further collapse of the boxes.

Just here the conductor called "Pond Street!" and the girl, looking up wildly, cried, "Oh, stop the car, please! I want to get out here."

Raising my hat I begged her to allow me to assist, and forthwith seized one cat by the neck, entangled in a chaos of string and smashed pasteboard, and followed her, grasping the other beast in a like condition.

She thought I meant merely to help her off the car, and turned to thank me and take my cat. But already I had signaled the gaping conductor to leave us, for I saw that she was perfectly helpless here in this wilderness alone with those two ferocious wild beasts, for the boxes no longer made any pretense to contain them. What else was there for me to do?

"Oh, now you have lost your car," she said regretfully, "and you were so kind to help me."

"Not at all," I replied. "You could not manage these animals alone. You must let me help you carry them wherever you are going."

She opened her lips as if to speak. She looked at me doubtfully, then at the struggling cats which we each held at arm's length, and saw the folly of refusing my offer.

"I was taking them to the Home," she volunteered simply.

"I beg your pardon," I queried in stupid perplexity— *"the Home?"*

"Yes, the home for stray cats; it is somewhere on this street. These are both stray cats. I had to take them in, but I couldn't keep them, poor things—I have three already," she went on to explain with sweet compassion.

"I should say not," I assented fervently, as the gray villain I held began to struggle and scratch afresh in frantic efforts to regain his straydom. She looked reproachful. We had begun slowly to climb the hilly street with our forlorn burdens, she evidently still hesitating whether to allow me the precious trust. For some steps we walked silently, for the situation was just a little difficult, and I could find no remark sufficiently *apropos*. I could feel her eyes scan me covertly as we went, though I kept mine diligently upon the contortions of the beast which I held. And, internally, I was laughing at the absurdity of the situation, and wondering what the boys would say to see me now.

At last she turned to me with a solemn little pucker in her forehead. "This is very unconventional," she began hesitatingly, "and I don't know that I ought to let you help me, Mr.—ah—"

"Smith," I prompted her. She raised her eyebrows, and looked at me oddly, and I saw that she believed it to be an *alias,* which frightened her.

"But there is nothing else for you to do," I assured her earnestly. "It may be unconventional, but it's common sense. I will do all I can to help you and to find these poor creatures a home." I tried to look affectionately at the cats. "Do you know where this home is, Miss—er—er—"

She hesitated a moment, then her eyes twinkled. "Miss Jones," she said. I saw at once that she had not given me her real name, though I had been more frank. But again I caught that half veiled expression in her face of amusement and secret understanding. She puzzled me.

She had launched into a vivid and enthusiastic description of this charitable refuge for homeless cats and dogs, and I was growing quite interested in the same, when, with a mighty effort, the black cat which she was carrying kicked himself free of her arm, and was off like an inky streak.

"Oh, catch him!" she cried, turning piteously to me. "Do catch him, Mr. Smith!"

Her tone was not to be resisted, and another moment saw me in the chase. The other cat which I held under my arm grew frantic at my pace, and struggled madly with my ill-protected flesh. But I heeded not. Such a chase! Over hill, over dale, through bush and especially briar, over park and dale and stone wall into a pasture I pursued the wretched creature. I might be chasing him to this day but for the tangled mess of string and pasteboard—once a box tied by a girl—which he dragged after him, and which at last caught in a bush and anchored him hard and fast to wait for me. I grasped him by the scruff of his neck and breathed in his tattered ear some words not calculated to soothe his wounded spirits; then, with a beast under each arm, I strode triumphantly back to where on the brow of the hill Miss Jones waited anxiously and appreciatively for me.

"Oh, you are so kind," she faltered as I came up. "How can I ever thank you? Here is your hat; I went for it over in the field."

I told her of course that I was sufficiently thanked already, as I sat on the stone wall recovering my breath, while she bent over me trying to untangle the graceless cats from their harnesses, and from one another, and from me.

The spirit of our adventure was fast sweeping away the barrier of conventional restraint and her evident feeling of wrong-doing. It was with admirable *sangfroid* that at my suggestion she reached in my vest pocket for my jack knife with which to cut the tangle of cord and pasteboard from the struggling animals.

She laughed aloud at the spectacle which I presented, and I know it must have been an unusually picturesque one, sitting there breathless, and hatless, but, alas! far from catless.

"Patience on a Monument," she laughed.

"If you will represent Grief, I think I can feel it worthwhile to smile at her," I remarked with a feeble attempt to illustrate my words.

"Oh, don't smile," she hastened to add. "It was so much funnier before when you glared so tragically at the poor cats, Jer—Mr. Smith."

I almost thought she was going to say something else. But how could she know my name was Jerome? It must have been imagination. And yet again, I caught that half-familiar look which once more set me to puzzling my brain in vain.

We again took up our line of march, Miss Jones gathering up the black cat in both arms, and I holding the gray one less tenderly but quite as firmly. Thus, with encouraging comments to one another, and amid wails of protest from the ungrateful cats, we proceeded for nearly half a mile till we came to a quaint little lonely structure, which from environing sympathetic sounds we judged to be the Home.

We walked boldly up to the front door, and I managed to ring the electric bell with my elbow. We waited; no response . I rang again—an even longer peal. Still no one came with open arms to receive our contributions. Separating, we went around opposite corners of the building hoping to find another entrance. At the rear were sundry sheds and wooden barracks, whence issued plaintive mews and barks, and outside a second door in the main building I found a printed sign which read: "Closed to visitors on Saturdays and Sundays. No animals received after 2:00 P.M. on Saturday."

Miss Jones had come up and was reading the sign over my shoulder. I took out my watch—it was half-past four. She looked up at me in despair.

"What shall I do?" she asked.

I looked at Miss Jones; I looked at her cat, and at mine; I looked about me, and a fiendish thought entered my mind. There was a placid sheet of water at the foot of the hill. It was not for nothing that Pond Street was so named, and chosen as a site for the Home. But as my eyes wandered toward this solution of the problem that interested me, they met those of Miss Jones's, and she frowned sternly. Possibly the bare thought may have occurred to her also.

"No!" she said, as if answering a word which indeed I had never spoken. "No! I will never desert them now. I will neither leave them here, since we can't get in, nor turn them loose, poor things, to starve; and certainly I will not have them—made away with." She glanced toward the pond. "No! I must find homes for them out here. There must be someone who would love to have such beautiful kitties."

I looked at the two miserable specimens in silence, but it was not the silence of assent.

"But—why, you must have some engagement," she said, as if this possibility had just occurred to her. "I must not bother you any longer—er—Mr. Smith. You have been so awfully kind already."

Her gratitude was charming; she had beautiful brown eyes. I assured her that I had no engagement. Indeed, Aunt Dosia never knew how near she came to the great happiness of my company.

"But," I went on, "you simply can't carry both those cats," and Malkin gave a howl of anguish.

"Oh, yes I could," she replied, but somewhat doubtfully, as Tom voiced a contradictory and very profane sentiment.

"No," I said firmly, "as you won't desert the cats, Miss Jones, so I will never desert you until you have disposed of them to suit yourself."

It was a rash promise, but I was now thoroughly interested in the game. Even playing knight-errant to homeless cats (and a pretty girl) was better than an afternoon with Aunt Dosia.

Accordingly, we descended the hill again to the more thickly settled street on the car line, proffering our wares to all whom we met, and I at least feeling extremely silly. For people eyed us with a surprised and disapproving stare, or received our advances with amusement and derision. No one seemed to take us or our forlorn burdens seriously, and at last Miss Jones grew much discouraged.

"I don't believe it's any use to speak to the passersby," she said, despondently, "they are so unsympathetic. Let us call at the houses along this street. You go on that side, and I on this, and see who will succeed first."

The plan did not sound attractive; the whole charm of the adventure was in sharing it with her and being in her company. But I had pledged my allegiance, and she was the captain of the enterprise. So we separated, and I began my visitations.

And this was the result of my knight-errantry! Imagine me hawking a disreputable tom-cat about from door to door. I have never envied a book agent's life, but his must be paradise compared to that of a stray cat peddler. We wandered, it seemed, for miles, with only contumely and rebuff or ribald comment for our pains. But at last I found a wan and guileless old maid who looked with favor upon my suit and relieved me of the gray villain who was just the color of her hair. Cheerfully I resigned my trust, and then swinging my cramped and lacerated arms in long unfelt freedom, I looked about for Miss Jones. She was some distance back on the other side, and had evidently not yet been successful. It was nearly six o'clock, and I had had no dinner, but I had promised not to desert her; and besides, I wanted to see this thing through. I believed it could be written up into a funny story that would pay me for all my sufferings; but I waited for a more picturesque *denouement*.

So I rejoined her who was tired and despairing and chagrined at my success. Tom himself seemed broken spirited at his unpopularity, and now lay passive and meek in her embrace. Together once more we visited many doors, but at last we found a little girl who persuaded her mamma to let her keep the black monster. Heaven grant that he has not ere now broken her kindly, unsuspecting little heart.

With a sigh of relief, Miss Jones descended the long flight of steps and looked smilingly up at me. I felt as if we were old friends. Our adventure had established quite a comradeship between us.

"Well, that is a good job done," she said, "and I think they will really be happier than they would have been in the Home, don't you?"

"Yes, doubtless it is better—for the *cats*," I replied significantly. She frowned.

"They were very nice cats," she retorted.

"Yes, indeed—I have nothing against them," I answered promptly. "On the contrary, I owe them a very interesting and thrilling afternoon, and a most pleasant acquaintance with—Miss Jones."

Her face changed immediately, and a return to conventional dignity took the place of her simple freedom of hitherto.

"And now, when I have thanked you most heartily for your very great kindness, Mr. Smith," she said primly, "I will bid you good afternoon. I am going to town on this next car."

"So am I," I began boldly, but I stopped at the almost frightened look on her face.

"You—you mustn't," she said quickly. "We—we are strangers, you know, after all. I really—you know you promised as soon as the cats were disposed of—"

I argued in vain about this absurd convention of society. She was firm, and I had to give in.

"Very well," I said sadly. "I will leave you then; but really, Miss Jones, I must take this car too, for I have to get back to the city, and you know it is rather late."

She saw the implied reproach, for I had wasted a whole afternoon upon her blessed cats, and it was now nearly dark.

"Well—then you must sit at the other end of the car, please," she insisted. "I know I am doing only what is right to ask you this." She was adorably confused and troubled, and so of course I had to agree to this also, absurd as it was. We formally said Goodbye, on the corner, and she thanked me very prettily again. Then the car came, and she entered by the rear platform, while I got on in front and sat down in a corner diagonally opposite. What an absurd situation? Here we were in the car together as when we came out, but with what hours of common history, what experience, what a bond of sympathy between us! And yet I must not speak to her or know her again if we should meet. I rebelled at the silly convention which kept us apart, and was closing the door already half open between us.

I could hardly restrain a broad smile as I met by merest accident her own twinkling glance, immediately withdrawn. I saw I must occupy myself, or I could not keep my eyes from her, she was altogether so sweet and conscious and charming. So

I drew out my pad and began to jot down my story of the afternoon's happenings. As I scribbled I became absorbed in recalling the thrilling events past, and we had almost reached my own street when, happening to glance up, I found Miss Jones looking steadily in my direction; but as I caught her eye she colored and hastily closed a little notebook in which she seemed to have been writing.

Goodness! I thought. *Could she be a scribbler too, with like intent?* But just here she signaled the car to stop, and with a stiffening of the neck and an evident intention not to look at me again, she alighted. However, just as the car moved on, almost involuntarily she turned her head and once more I caught a last gleam of fun and gratitude from her sweet eyes. Then she was gone.

I wrote my story, the bare facts needing no exaggeration to make them amusing; but I invented a touching and sentimental *finale,* that of my own adventure seeming strangely inadequate and commonplace. But when finished, I dared not send the article to my own paper—it was too probable that Miss Jones would see it, and that would never do. I had expressed myself pretty freely in my description of her, and besides—I feared she would not appreciate that conclusion. For the same reason, I dared not send it to any very well known magazine. But I remembered that a modest little periodical, *The Autocrat,* had been started in my own native town of Shefton, which I had not visited for several years, and I sent my story there. It was promptly accepted.

For weeks I was haunted by the puzzling familiarity of Miss Jones's face. And yet—knowing that this was not her real name, I did not see how I could ever manage to meet her and gain an introduction. It was maddening, for I had never wanted anything so much in all my life as to renew our acquaintance.

I haunted the street into which I had seen her disappear, in hopes of at least learning her address, but in vain.

One morning three weeks later, I received a copy of *The Autocrat.* I scanned the pages eagerly for my story—for even my own history of that afternoon with "Miss Jones" seemed precious to me. I found the article and was pleased to see that they had illustrated it. But what! How the deuce! I looked at the first picture a second time. It was I myself, the very image, helping Miss Jones herself from the car, with the two cats as natural and ugly as life, between us. What did it mean? I turned the pages. Yes, there was I, hatless and undignified—the artist was no flatterer—scouring wildly after the escaping cat, the other hanging under my arm. Here we sat on the wall untangling the cats; here, two weary pilgrims, we despaired outside the Home; here was I, peddling cats from door to door, and lastly, our dignified return at opposite corners of the car. The whole story was told in a series of most clever pictures—it needed no words by

Jerome B. Smith to complete the tale. It was all there—except my *finale*. I noted that. And the illustrator? There was only one eye-witness who could have caught those sketches, and I remembered the little notebook. I searched for the name eagerly, and at last found it in a corner of one picture: "W. Irene Jones."

Her name was Jones then, after all. Hurrah! Now I could find her address from the publishers. Then a thought struck me: *Why had she also favored* The Autocrat? "W. Irene Jones"—all of a sudden I understood it all: her familiar face, the smile that haunted me. Why, I knew the girl! She was Winny Jones, of course, my little playmate of fifteen years before, whom I had not seen since I left Shefton. My little Winny, whom as a boy of twelve I had carried piggyback, and teased and kissed and romped with, a baby of five. And now that I thought of it, I remembered that when I was last in Shefton, they had said she'd come to Boston to study art.

I lost no time, you may be sure, in learning Winny's address; and not two hours later I was waiting for her in a pretty little studio on St. Botolph Street.

She entered with flushed cheeks and her eyes laughing to match the corners of her pretty mouth. She held my card in her hand.

"So it was your real name after all," she said, as she stretched out her hand cordially. "I thought—"

"So did I," I interrupted eagerly.

"I thought," she went on, "that it might be a false name, but I was almost sure it was really you. For you see I remembered you, though it has been so long."

"But why the dickens didn't you say so, then?" I asked half impatiently.

She pouted: "Why—you didn't recognize me, and I was provoked. I wasn't going to be the only one to remember."

"But a girl changes so much more than a man in ten years," I apologized. "You were only a little girl when I left, and even your name is different now. I used to call you Winny."

"And I almost called you 'Jerry' lots of times that afternoon, just as I used to," she laughed. "But I tried to be awfully dignified, so you wouldn't guess." And so we chatted happily about the events of that wonderful day, and she told me how she had sent the sketches to *The Autocrat*, as a joke on me, for she was sure I would see them.

"And call?" I boldly hinted. But she indignantly scorned the imputation, and we almost quarreled. Then I asked what she thought of my *finale*. She flushed a delicious rosy pink.

"It was impossible—an altogether far-fetched and improbable ending," she declared emphatically.

"Oh, no, I don't think so," I rejoined. "I think it very natural and just what the story needed to make it end well. Don't you like stories to end well?"

We argued the matter for some time from a literary standpoint, and later we touched upon it from other standpoints. And in the end I succeeded in convincing her. So it happened that our adventure finally did "end well" after all. And I hope each of those cats has as happy a home as I now enjoy—thanks to them and to our tour of the four.

* * * * *

"The Tour of the Four," by Abbie Farwell Brown. Published in The Ladies' World, *June 1898. Abbie Farwell Brown was a prolific writer of short stories, novels, and poetry around the turn of the twentieth century.*

STINKY, THE SKUNK THAT WOULDN'T LEAVE

Tony Ortiz

A skunk is a small critter, and a man is a giant in comparison. In spite of that apparent imbalance of power, there is a level playing field between them.

Perhaps I ought to qualify that statement a bit . . .

* * * * *

Several weeks before this manuscript was due at Pacific Press®, our son Greg and his boyhood pal, Tony Ortiz, spent a week with us. During that visit, as we shared memories, Tony told us this story, in which his father, Yddo, played a not-quite-leading role, and his mother, Brenda, a strong supporting role.

Yddo, born in Colombia, was in his midteens when his sister brought him to the U.S.; consequently, he and the English language have had a lifelong tug-of-war. Hence his Yddo-isms have become legendary; as has been true of his tremendous shock of bushy black hair. In this story, Tony has done his best to transcribe his father's speech and recreate his father's appearance and mannerisms.

Never before that day had we known that Tony was such a master storyteller. As he relived this story, we laughed until it hurt. We wouldn't let Tony return to Florida until he promised to write it down for us. He enlisted the assistance of his father and mother in fleshing out the complete story. Just two days before the manuscript for this book was due, Tony e-mailed us the story. There was no question but that it had to anchor this collection!

* * * * *

A number of years ago, in the outskirts of a little town known as Keene, about thirty miles south of Fort Worth, Texas, Mom and Dad bought an old farmhouse. It was not, to put it mildly, a pretty sight. No small thanks to the passing of time, neglect, and fierce Texas winds, the forlorn wooden house leaned in every imaginable direction. Driving up the then hot, dusty gravel road, you were greeted with a roof sagging like a hammock, bleached-white paint peeling off the sun-stained siding, sprinkles of white paint splotching the brown grass like snow, and waist-high tumbleweeds made it difficult to even get to the house.

It took months for our family to transition from suburbia to quiet country living. In time, all working together, we transformed the wreck into a home. And Mom would, more often than not, say, "You should have seen this old house when God had it all to Himself."

Time passed, and we settled into rural routine. For us kids, the chickens and cows had to be fed, the woodbin had to be filled with firewood, and our other chores completed, before we were permitted to head off to school. Only then was Mom able to relax a bit and enjoy quiet country life.

Was able to. On one never-to-be-forgotten morning, Mom was standing in the middle of the kitchen taking a much-needed break, when her peace was broken by the sound of wild animals fighting. The screeching, squalling, snarling, and hissing escalated as the fight became more intense. Suddenly, Mom was engulfed by a rising cloud of smog. As the smoldering cloud reached her now tearing eyes, a not quite celestial moment occurred: the realization that the most odiferous of animals had staked a claim to the house. Evidently, the skunk [it turned out to be female] had begun a fight with the family cat under the house, below the kitchen where Mom was standing. Concluding that she was losing ground to the much larger cat, the skunk called in reinforcements: whipping up her tail and decommissioning her enemy below with one blast—getting two for the price of one by nailing Mom in the kitchen above as well. Mom made a dash for the old bathroom toilet and threw up her morning breakfast, two or three times.

As you may know, old houses like this were built without a solid foundation; they floated on beams and cinder blocks. At some point, this momma skunk and her family had created a home under our home. Frustrated beyond belief that a skunk would actually spray the family home, Dad was furious and went out and bought many pounds of mothballs. Placing mothballs around the perimeter of the house, he boasted on how that skunk would die in this tomb of mothballs. As it turned out, there were no other skunk incidents that spring.

However, the story doesn't stop there. The following spring, while we were all out of the house, the skunk attacked again—a well-planned attack from different corners of the house. So we all ganged together to salvage what we could. The house was totally fumigated, and we were forced to throw out our clothes, rugs, drapes, and sheets. The stuff we just couldn't bear to part with, we hung in the rafters of our carport in the vain hope that someday our things might outlast their distinctive fragrance. Instead, it was a gift that just kept giving: long afterwards, the family celebrated getting away from it all by taking a ski trip to Colorado. What a joy it was to breathe the fresh clean cool air of the Rockies! At least it was . . . until we unpacked our ski clothes—and the stench was so bad we had to evacuate the lodge!

Once again, Dad went on the warpath, consulting all the authorities on skunk-eradication he could round up. Folks at the local pest control store enthusiastically recommended a special spray guaranteed to "take the skunk smell away forever."

(Country Lesson 101, FYI—*nothing* takes away skunk spray odor forever.) Nevertheless, as rookie rednecks, we bought barrels of the stuff and coated down the whole house. What a job we did: the car, couches, chairs, socks, underwear, napkins, washclothes . . . everything. My sister Kelly even sprayed her wrists and dabbed a little behind the ear like perfume. She must have thought it smelled better than skunk.

To this day, we have no idea what we sprayed all over ourselves and the house. It most likely was a mixture of garlic, Ajax, baking soda, Coca-Cola, and what could have been some very old rotten pinto beans (maybe even some gasoline) . . . well, at least it smelled somewhat better than skunk.

Another source of information was our neighbor Keith Montgomery. Now, Keith was about thirteen years old at the time, and also known in our house for having the longest Texas *deeerrraaaawwwl* in the county. As a religious man, my father wasn't about to kill anything under the sun. He would try to reason with a snake if it would listen. All it took was a few simple words from Keith: "I would never let some rodent skunk take my family and spray them over like that, *whyyy,* I would put a bullet right between the eyes of that Black-and-White." That was all my dad needed to defend his manhood: hearing a thirteen-year-old tell him the skunk was the real head of the house. At that time, Dad couldn't picture himself killing anything and quickly dismissed the idea. After all, he still hoped the skunk would pull out and move out on her own.

Sure enough, gone but not forgotten, the skunk was not talked about again until the beginning of the next spring. Dad, a.k.a. General Patton, was seen preparing the house for what looked to be a war. With a hammer and a bucket of nails, you could hear him from inside, learning the new art of working and mumbling to himself. "I'mgoingtogetdatdirtyrottensmellywodent. . . ." Sure enough, Dad's little job of art couldn't hold a calm breeze. The skunk had burrowed a hole under the boards and was once again living in the basement she called the Ritz-Carlton.

Good for us, because we made preparations. We may not have been the smartest kids in Texas, but we weren't dumb. As soon as word spread throughout the family, we all headed to Grandma's—except for Dad. He just couldn't believe the skunk had made her way back under the house. The rest of us moved to town, where we all dressed and showered at Grandma's until the skunk received her pink slip.

One particular Sabbath morning, none of us will ever forget: We all got ready for church at Grandma's, then headed to church. Dad had agreed to meet us there. Here we'd sit together, next to the aisle under the balcony. We got there first that morning. Dad was late—but not late enough; he walked down the center aisle and sat down with us in our designated family pew, giving new meaning to the term. As he did so, we parted as quickly as though he were a hand grenade rather than our father. Unbeknownst to him, during the night the skunk had sprayed his closet from below. The funny thing—but not to Dad—was that when a skunk gives your house a nocturnal spraying, since you unconsciously breathe it all night, in the morning nothing seems different from the day before. Just as is true with those who work at a perfume counter, you lose your ability to differentiate between smells.

So it was that morning: Dad had sashayed into church smelling like a skunk. The couple in the pew just in front of us (George and Sharon Shaw) swiveled around, looked at Dad, sniffed, touched their noses—and gagged. We all missed church that day, and all together and with one voice recommended a bath of Skunk-Off for Dad. Poor Dad: frustrated, angry, lost, evicted from family, bewildered, and mostly just plain embarrassed, all the tears in the world wouldn't have erased his sense of shame and determination to get that skunk!

Being that Dad was the local photographer, later that evening he'd promised a bride and groom to take their wedding pictures. Every time he'd raise the camera to his face to take a photo, he'd breathe in. Even in his impaired olfactory state, he belatedly realized that his camera too had become a carrier of skunk. Later, when the wedding photos were developed and he studied them, to his chagrin he noted wrinkled noses in some of the photographs. So he couldn't help but wonder what the heck the bride and groom must have thought.

* * * * *

Years passed, and every spring, regular as clockwork, Momma Skunk let us know she had no intention of surrendering the house to us.

Dad tried *everything*: somewhere he'd heard that skunks couldn't swim, so he rigged up a convoluted Rube Goldberg contraption that consisted of a ten-gallon bucket complete with a climb-friendly rodent ramp. The general idea was to fill the bucket with water, sprinkle sardines as bait in the water, then wait for Momma Skunk to toddle up the ramp to the top of the bucket and be so entranced by the sight of all those transplanted sardines that she'd fall in and drown attempting to round them up. At least that was Dad's plan, but the ungrateful skunk would have nothing to do with Dad's artfully crafted rodent ramp and death bucket.

One particular year, in his desperation, Dad forsook his lifelong noncombatancy and knocked on our other neighbor's door, and bluntly asked, "DjuhaveagunIkinborrow?" At that time, Dad didn't know the first thing about a gun, rifle, or slingshot, for that matter. Willing to bring closure to the siege of the Ortiz family, Mr. Kouns spent the entire day giving Dad a crash course in guns, showing him repeatedly how to load, unload, and shoot a shotgun.

That very night Dad jubilantly planned for Ms. Skunk's funeral. After making himself a celebrative sandwich, popping some popcorn, and preparing a big thermos of hot chocolate, he sallied out to battle with his snacks, a blanket, the borrowed shotgun, climbed up on the roof of the house, and settled down for battle.

The neighbors were impressed with Dad's new militancy, as for three long spring nights the war went on. Each morning, they assumed Texas would be minus one live skunk. Instead, the only things lost turned out to be sleep and buckshot. About twice each night we could hear Dad as he sneaked, crawled, slid, and schooched [Southern term for dragging your butt along the edge so you don't fall] along the roof's edge, then tiptoed to the presumed proper position, and tried to get the best angle to shred that black and white critter into confetti. Finally, a shot so loud the sound shook the house! Next morning, Dad had to admit that the only result of his blast was that now a wounded skunk, with buckshot in her butt, was living under our house.

When *that* didn't work, Mr. Kouns came up with another solution. Somewhere he'd heard that skunks would refuse to live in any place that was lighted, so Dad gathered together so many strings of Christmas lights that at night, while the upper part of our house was dark, there was such a terrific glow blazing out from below the house I swear you could have seen our house from the moon! In fact it was so bright we had to pull the drapes before we could sleep ourselves! Now Dad was certain Momma Skunk would pack her bags and leave. But when she didn't, Dad groused,

"That darned" [I'm afraid, as religious a man as he was and is, he used a stronger word than *darned*] . . . "Dadt—skunkmustagoneoutandboughtherselfsunglasses!"

* * * * *

Still ticked off at her assailant, Momma Skunk didn't even wait until spring the following year. In a surprise night attack, she sprayed the house from below. Mom woke us up early to explain this unexpectedly early opening of hostilities. We'd slept through it all and never smelled a thing. Since we couldn't smell anything different, we decided to go to school anyhow. After all, we still had plenty of "Skunk Spray" left over from the previous season—it ought to still work.

By 9:00 A.M. that morning, a little third-grade girl had already called her mother, crying. She'd been teased nonstop by classmates and wanted to come home. By this time, I had one school building smelling like skunk, and Kelly had taken care of the other; by now the entire elementary school smelled like skunk. When Mom got there to pick up her daughter, there she was, with Benny Lee pinned to the floor, beating him with his own shoe, screaming at the top of her lungs, "And don't call me Stinky anymore!"

Meanwhile, Dad was busy setting up traps in the backyard. All our pets were shut inside the house for Dad didn't want *them* to be caught in traps. He angrily placed fresh bait in the traps each night in the hopes that *this time* he'd finally take care of that pestiferous varmint. Yeah, right: Momma Skunk grew fat that year. Each morning, when Dad checked the traps, they'd be empty. Dad began to develop a permanent scowl across his brow. *Beaten, defeated, angered, depressed, frustrated,* and *disbelieving,* are just a few pertinent adjectives reflecting Dad's condition that year, grousing that he might have had better luck with a bear or rhinoceros.

By the last of April, Dad had turned deadly serious: he bought a .22 revolver. He sealed the outside of the house with every skunk-defying thing he could lay his hands on: Kevlar, cast-iron, barbed-wire, and most anything else he could find that might work. Only one tiny little opening in a piece of tin was left open. Dad had everything planned so that it was foolproof: the opening was directly under his bedroom window; when he heard the tin crinkle, he'd grab the revolver on his nightstand, make a bee-line for the backdoor—and "Goodbye skunk!"

Early next morning, Mom was midway through preparing breakfast when she chanced to look out the window, and there was Ms. Skunk gazing on what she considered her property. Dad was in the midst of a deep springtime dream, having slept through any skunk-generated night-noises, when he was awakened by a news tidbit from Mom: "Yddo, your black and white friend is relaxing in the backyard."

"Thatlittlecockroachbettersayveryquickprayer," announced Dad, leaping out of bed and grabbing his weapon from the nightstand, then rushing out into the early morning dew, ready to prove once and for all that a new sheriff was in town. Forget clothes: real men don't waste time on nonessentials.

For the watchers inside the house, it didn't take long to discover that Dad was neither John Wayne nor Clint Eastwood—it was more like watching Don Knotts or Tim Conway. Bristly black bed-headed hairdo, white underwear, and white T-shirt, there stood Dad pointing his gun at the skunk grazing calmly not ten feet away. *Bang! Bang!* . . . Dad looked down the barrel of the gun—not exactly the smartest thing to do with a loaded gun—muttering "Whatsamattawichju? Where-daheckaredabullets?" He'd now missed at point-blank range—twice! Though we knew Dad wasn't a crack marksman, one wouldn't think it would take much skill to shoot a skunk from the same distance as the remote to the television. Adjusting his sights, using both hands now—since his first one-handed quick-draw cowboy experiences didn't seem to have the special effect he was looking for: *Bang! Bang! Bang!* . . . From the window, we could see him mouthing the words, "Whatsawrongwid-disestupidgun?"

Eye to eye they faced each other—obviously, this was not how the West was won. As we watched, there crouched Dad in skivvies and T-shirt, knees slightly bent, weight firmly on the balls of his feet, looking like Elmer Fudd determined to make big things happen. *Bang!* . . . *Click* . . . *Click* . . . *Click.* The six-shooter, having now given its all in a losing cause, could only make clicky sounds. But, not to worry, there was still one more thing to do that would save the day! Dad wound up like Nolan Ryan and threw, with all his might, his empty pistol at the skunk—and *missed.*

Have you ever seen a happy skunk? This little combatant was so deliriously happy, she did a little four-legged tap-dance before placing both front paws firmly on the ground, lifting her hind-legs into a euphoric handstand, and wisping her tail up and over, before she sprayed Dad in the middle of his T-shirted chest—a bull's-eye by skunk standards. To this day, when Dad retells the story, he declares it was—other than the stench, of course—really rather a pleasant experience: like warm misty air hitting his chest from a leaf blower.

But when Dad finally woke to his true condition, he forsook his assailant and ignominiously fled toward the sliding glass doors. "Not on your life!" I muttered to myself as I raced to lock every door in the house. As it turned out, I locked the sliding glass door a millisecond before Dad reached for it. If Dad was angry before, being locked out by his son raised his condition to beyond livid, and he opened his hands against the glass to plead his case, accompanied by, "WhatsamattawidjuDony?" [he pronounced my name "Donee"]. To my everlasting shame, I merely pointed in the direction of town and mouthed, "Go to Grandma's—we're going back to bed."

But soft-hearted Mom took mercy on the vanquished warrior. She jumped in the car and raced off to the nearest foodstore. When she returned, she had a towel around her head and nose like Lawrence of Arabia. Since we hadn't been able to sleep, we now watched as Mom drenched in tomato juice our family hero. After which Dad, resembling the perpetrator of a horrendously bloody crime, grabbed a shovel and buried his shirt and underwear in the backyard. His eyes were bloodshot, his face pale as tomato juice would permit, and his head repeatedly jerked like a cat coughing up hairballs. Then we turned away, for we really didn't want to see what was coming up next.

Mom maintains that that very afternoon, Dad called Carson's Pest Control with an urgent request to "bring out a twenty-pound steak, sprinkle it with sleeping powder, or something stronger, and toss it into our backyard."

They did, and that's how we finally got our house back.

* * * * *

Mercifully, the curtains now close on the epic showdown between Ms. Skunk and Mr. Ortiz.

* * * * *